T0299059

Problems in Portfolio Theory and the Fundamentals of Financial Decision Making

World Scientific Series in Finance
(ISSN: 2010-1082)

World Scientific Series
in FINANCE vol. 10

Problems in Portfolio Theory
and the Fundamentals of
Financial Decision Making

Leonard C. MacLean
Dalhousie University, Canada

William T. Ziemba
University of British Columbia, Canada
London School of Economics, UK

World Scientific

JERSEY · LONDON · SINGAPORE · BEIJING · SHANGHAI · HONG KONG · TAIPEI · CHENNAI · TOKYO

Published by

World Scientific Publishing Co. Pte. Ltd.
5 Toh Tuck Link, Singapore 596224
USA office: 27 Warren Street, Suite 401-402, Hackensack, NJ 07601
UK office: 57 Shelton Street, Covent Garden, London WC2H 9HE

Library of Congress Cataloging-in-Publication Data
Names: MacLean, Leonard C., author. | Ziemba, W. T., author.
Title: Problems in portfolio theory and the fundamentals of financial decision making /
    authored by Leonard C. MacLean and William T. Ziemba.
Description: Hackensack, NJ : World Scientific Pub. Co. Pte. Ltd., 2017. |
    Series: World Scientific series in finance, ISSN 2010-1082 ; Vol. 10 | Includes index.
Identifiers: LCCN 2016022160| ISBN 9789814759144 | ISBN 9789814749930
Subjects: LCSH: Portfolio management. | Investments. | Finance. | Decision making.
Classification: LCC HG4529.5 .M33 2017 | DDC 332.601--dc23
LC record available at https://lccn.loc.gov/2016022160

British Library Cataloguing-in-Publication Data
A catalogue record for this book is available from the British Library.

Desk Editor: Lum Pui Yee

Typeset by Stallion Press
Email: enquiries@stallionpress.com

Printed in Singapore

DEDICATION

To my wife, Dr Sandra L. Schwartz, who not only suggested this problems book but also helped produce it.

Dr Maclean dedicates this volume to the Herbert Lamb Trust in acknowledgement of financial support for his research.

PREFACE

The problems presented here can be used with the books Ziemba and Vickson, *Stochastic Optimization Models in Finance* and MacLean and Ziemba, *Handbook of The Fundamentals of Financial Decision Making*, the two sources with which these problems are associated. They cover many aspects of static and dynamic theory as well as other important subjects such as arbitrage and asset pricing, utility theory, stochastic dominance, risk aversion and static portfolio theory, risk measures, and dynamic portfolio theory and asset allocation, so the problems can be used with other important books that cover these topics. The problems presented are of two kinds. The first set are new problems relevant to various chapters of the MacLean–Ziemba edited *Handbook of the Fundamentals of Financial Decision Making*. The second set are problems modified from the Ziemba–Vickson book. Both sets of problems can also be used with other books and courses dealing with portfolio theory and related topics. Special thanks go to Haim Levy, Steve Mizusawa, Edward O. Thorp, Igor Evstigneev, W. Bahsoun, Michael Taksar, Sebastien Lleo and Mark Davis, who contributed problems associated with their papers in *The Fundamentals of Financial Decision Making Handbook*. Thanks also to Raymond G. Vickson who worked with William

T. Ziemba on the original 1975 version of Stochastic Optimization
Models in Finance.

Leonard C. MacLean

William T. Ziemba

May 2016

CONTENTS

BOOKS FOR WHICH THE PROBLEMS ARE DESIGNED

(a) *The Handbook of the Fundamentals of Financial Decision Making*, Leonard C. MacLean and William T. Ziemba (eds.), (2013)

Overview

The theory and practice of decision making in finance had a long and storied history. Many of the fundamental concepts in economics as well as the models in stochastic optimization have their origins in finance. In this handbook a selection of the key papers in financial decision making are brought together to provide a comprehensive picture of the components and methods. The handbook is composed of two volumes. Volume I consists of a collection of reprints of seminal papers on the foundations of decision making in finance. Volume II contains mostly original papers which explore aspects of decision models. A special emphasis is placed on models which optimize capital growth.

In Section A of Volume I, the concept of arbitrage is presented in a set of papers. Arbitrage is an opportunity for risk-free gains, and an absence of arbitrage is a condition for a stable financial market. The seminal paper is Ross (1976), where the Arbitrage Pricing Theory (APT) is introduced. He defines the prices on assets by a linear relation to common factors (latent random variables) each with expectation zero. After accounting for risk there is no price premium, that is, arbitrage does not exist. Another way of stating this condition is that after adjusting for risk, the price process is a martingale. The Fundamental Theorem of Asset Pricing states that "no arbitrage" is equivalent to the existence of an equivalent "martingale measure". The papers by Schachermayer (2010a,b) put the fundamental theorem in a general setting. There exists a martingale measure if and only if the price process satisfies a no free lunch with vanishing risk condition. The martingale measure is a risk-neutral measure and all assets have the same expected value (the risk-free rate) under the risk-neutral measure.

Kallio and Ziemba (2007) use theorems of the alternative from mathematical programming to establish the existence of risk neutral probabilities for the discrete time and discrete space price process. The equivalence between no arbitrage and the existence of a martingale measure is extended to markets with various imperfections.

The concept of utility as an expression of preference is developed in Section B. Fishburn's (1969) paper gives a succinct presentation of expected utility theory. With a set of assumptions over decision maker preferences, Fishburn establishes the existence of a utility function and subjective probability distribution such that rational individuals act as though they were maximizing expected utility. Expected utility allows for the fact that many individuals are risk averse, meaning that the individual would refuse a fair gamble (a fair gamble has an expected value of zero).

In expected utility theory, the utilities of outcomes are weighted by their probabilities. Machina (2004) describes non-expected utility. It has been shown that people overweight outcomes that are considered certain relative to outcomes which are merely probable. There have been a variety of proposals for dealing with the violation of the independence axiom and the linearity in probabilities. One approach is Prospect Theory proposed by Tversky and Kahneman (1974) and Kahneman and Tversky (1979, 1984). The value function is S-shaped, being convex for losses $(x < 0)$ and concave for gains $(x > 0)$.

Prospect Theory has its critics. The papers by Levy and Levy (2002, 2004) cast doubt on the S-shaped value function, based on experimental results. The basis of their analysis is stochastic dominance which orders random variables. The paper by Wakker (2003) reinforces the importance of probability weighting as well as the S-shaped value in prospect theory. He re-examines the experiments, showing that the S-shape is compatible with the data. Baltussen *et al.* (2006) provides experimental results supporting the usual risk averse (concave) function over either the S-shape or reverse S-shape.

In financial decision making the (investment, consumption) process is dynamic, with the alternatives consisting of wealth and consumption decisions at points in time. Kreps and Porteus (1979) considered the intertemporal consistency of utility for making dynamic decisions. Preferences at different times are linked by a temporal consistency axiom, so that decisions are consistent in the sense that revealed outcomes at a later time wouldn't invalidate the optimality of earlier decisions.

The paper by Epstein and Zin (1989) builds on the temporal utility form to define a recursive negative utility which incorporates intertemporal substitution and risk aversion separately. The Epstein–Zin utility contains many popular utility functions negative power utility as special cases.

In Section C, the preference for random variables with the order relations of stochastic dominance are considered. Hanoch and Levy (1969) show that stochastic dominance can be defined by classes of utilities as characterized by higher order derivatives of the utility, with $u^{(k)}$ being the kth derivative. The dominance described is for a single period, usually the final period of accumulated capital. However, the capital is accumulated from investments over time and the trajectory to final wealth could be important in the assessment of utility. Levy and Paroush (1974) extend the notions of stochastic dominance to the multi-period case. With additive utility the stochastic dominance result is extended to multiple periods. Levy and Paroush also consider the geometric process where the final return is the product of period returns and give necessary conditions for first order dominance.

Efficient investment strategies, where risk is minimized for specified return, are the topic of Section D. A major advantage of Markowitz' (1952) mean-variance analysis is the relative ease of computing optimal strategies and as such it is a practical technique. The paper by Ziemba *et al.* (1974) consider the general risk-return investment problem for which they propose a two-step approach: the first step is to find the proportions invested in risky assets using a fractional program; the second step is to determine the optimal ratios of risky to non-risky assets.

Ziemba (1975) considered the computation of optimal portfolios when returns have a symmetric stable distribution. The normal is a stable distribution when the variance is finite, but the stable family is more general with dispersion replacing variance and has four rather than two parameters.

The utility function in the investment models is concave to reflect risk aversion. There are aspects of risk aversion, which are not captured by concavity. In the paper by Pratt (1964) an additional property of utility, decreasing absolute risk aversion, is introduced.

Rubinstein (1973) developed a measure of global risk aversion in the context of a parameter-preference equilibrium relationship. Some properties of this measure in the context of risk aversion with changing initial wealth levels appear in Kallberg and Ziemba (1983). They establish an important property of the global risk measure: Investors with the same R have the same optimal portfolios even with different wealth levels and utility functions.

Chopra and Ziemba (1993) consider the relative impact of estimation errors and the impact of risk aversion on portfolio performance, with the estimate of mean return being most important. MacLean, Foster and Ziemba (2007) use a Bayesian framework to include the covariance in an estimate of the mean. In essence, the return on one asset provides information about the return on related assets, and the sharing of information through the covariance improves the quality of estimates.

Expected utility is not the best theory for many risk attitudes, and does not explain the modest-scale risk aversion observed in practice. Rabin (2000) and Rabin and Thaler (2001) propose that a better explanation incorporates the concepts of loss aversion and mental accounting. They argue that loss aversion and the tendency to isolate each risky choice must both be components of a theory of risk attitudes.

The basic components of risk are (i) the chance of a potential loss and (ii) the size of the potential loss a lot of a Hantion has be focused on the value of loss at a specified probability: VaR (Jorion, 2006). Föllmer and Knispel (2013) view the financial risk of X as the capital requirement $\rho(X)$ to make the position X acceptable. With reference to acceptance sets, Rockafellar and Ziemba (2000) have established the following result: There is a one-to-one correspondence between acceptance sets A_ρ and the risk measures ρ.

The concept of capital requirement to cover the losses from investment captures the financial risk idea, but the probability of loss is not taken into account. Details on measures which use the distribution are provided in the papers of Krokhmal *et al.* (2011) and Föllmer and Knispel (2013). There is a one-to-one relationship between averse risk measures and deviation risk measures.

A variation is to consider the average of the values at risk (AVaR). Föllmer and Knispel show how AVaR is a building block for law-invariant risk measures. Since convexity is the desired property of a risk measure, the class of convex risk measures is considered in Föllmer and Knispel (2013), following Rockafellar and Ziemba (2000). Föllmer and Knispel (2013) also raise the issue of model uncertainty or model ambiguity. They discuss a robustification where the probability measure P is a member of a class $\wp$.

Markowitz's mean-variance analysis approach is generalized in Krokhmal *et al.* (2011). They present the decision problem as a trade-off between risk and reward, where a weighted combination of risk and reward is optimized. The weight is viewed as penalty on risk.

An application with the use of the penalty parameter approach is provided by the financial planning model InnoALM for the Austrian pension fund of the electronics firm Siemens, developed in Geyer and Ziemba (2008). The model uses a multi-period stochastic linear programming approach.

There are numerous models for investment choice in a stochastic dynamic environment and some are presented in Section F. Campbell *et al.* (2003) propose a standard first order autoregressive model for log-returns, with the inclusion of state variables in the dynamics. The Epstein–Zin recursive utility is used. With a log-linearization, the approximate optimal portfolio rule is the sum of two terms: a myopic component from the vector of excess returns (log optimal solution), and an intertemporal hedging component, which accounts for the fact that asset returns are state dependent and thereby time varying.

The returns from securities are related to the efficient operation of firms. The efficiency of a firm's operation can be analyzed from financial ratios, and firm efficiency related to market returns. Edirisinghe *et al.* (2013) in their paper look at firm input dimensions and output dimensions from an efficiency perspective — maximum output for a given level of input. A Data Envelopment Analysis calculates relative efficiency scores for firms from a linear programming model, and these scores are used in selection of securities for investment.

In a series of papers, Browne (1999b) considers a number of investment problems involving benchmarks. He determines a proportional strategy which maximizes the probability of exceeding a deterministic target. The strategy is equivalent to buying a European digital option with a particular strike and payoff. In the more general case of a stochastic benchmark, the optimal proportional strategy is composed of the benchmark and a hedging component. If the benchmark use the optimal growth strategy (Kelly), Browne (1999a) solves the probability maximizing problem for fixed T, finding a strategy that will beat the Kelly by an arbitrary percentage.

It is well known that features such as volatility of returns are time dependent. However, time periods can be segmented into regimes so that within a regime the distribution characteristics are stable. For example, the price and wealth dynamics may defined by geometric

Brownian motion within each regime, with the parameters being regime dependent. In this setup, the maximizing of the growth rate is analytic. These and other variations on the log utility model are described in MacLean and Ziemba (2013).

Some of the strongest properties of the optimal growth strategy relate to its evolutionary performance in an equilibrium capital market. In a frictionless market (no transactions costs) Bashoun *et al.* (2013) show that the Kelly rule is globally evolutionary stable, meaning that any other essentially different strategy will become extinct with probability 1. Davis and Lleo (2013) consider a variety of alternative models for price dynamics and determine the strategy which maximizes the power utility of wealth. The first variation is an intertemporal asset pricing model. The optimal portfolio invests in a fractional Kelly portfolio and cash. The fractional Kelly fund is a blend of funds: is a time dependent Kelly portfolio and an intertemporal hedging portfolio. Davis and Lleo also consider the pricing model where the diffusion is augmented by shocks, defined by a homogeneous Poisson process. They show that a model with shocks in the dynamics of returns and a negative power utility function of final wealth has an optimal portfolio strategy which has an option component. Browne (1999b) shows this is also true when the objective is maximizing the probability of beating a stochastic benchmark.

Thorp and Mizusawa (2013) consider the option component in two models for asset returns: log-normal, and fat tails. The strategies are a blend of stock and T-Bills versus the same blend of an option on stock and T-Bill.

Outline

Section A. Arbitrage and asset pricing

Kallio, M. and Ziemba, W. T. (2007). Using Tucker's theorem of the alternative to provide a framework for proving basic arbitrage results, *Journal of Banking and Finance* **31**: 2281–2302.

Ross, S. A. (1976). The arbitrage theory of capital asset pricing, *Journal of Economic Theory* **13**(3): 341–360.

Schachermayer, W. (2010a). The fundamental theorem of asset pricing, in *Encyclopedia* of *Quantitative Finance*, R. Cont (ed.), **2**: 792–801. New York: Wiley.
Schachermayer, W. (2010b). Risk neutral pricing, in *Encyclopedia of Quantitative Finance*, R. Cont (ed.), **4**: 1581–1585. New York: Wiley.

Section B. Utility theory

Baltussen, G., Post, T. and Vliet, P. V. (2006). Violations of cumulative prospect theory in mixed gambles with moderate probabilities, *Management Science* **52** (8): 1288–1290.
Epstein, L. G. and Zin, S. E. (1989). Substitution, risk aversion and the temporal behavior of consumption and asset returns: A theoretical framework, *Econometrica*, **57**(4): 937–969.
Fishburn, P. (1969). A general theory of subjective probabilities and expected utilities, *Annals of Mathematical Statistics* **40**(4): 1419–1429.
Kahneman, D. and Tversky, A. (1979). Prospect theory: An analysis of decisions under risk, *Econometrica* **47**(2), 263–291.
Kahneman, D. and Tversky, A. (1984). Choices, values, and frames, *American Psychologist* **39**(4): 341–350.
Kreps, D. M. and Porteus, E. L. (1979). Temporal von Neumann–Morgenstern and induced preferences, *Journal of Economic Theory* **20**(1): 81–109.
Levy, M. and Levy, H. (2002). Prospect theory: Much ado about nothing? *Management Science* **48**(10): 1334–1349.
Levy, M. and Levy, H. (2004). Prospect theory and mean-variance analysis, *Review of Financial Studies* **17**(4): 1015–1041.
Machina, M. (2004). Non-expected utility theory, in *Encyclopedia of Actuarial Science*, J. L. Teugels and B. Sundt (eds.), **2**: 1173–1179. New York: Wiley.
Rabin, M. (2000). Risk aversion and expected-utility theory: A calibration theorem, *Econometrica* **68**(5), 1281–1292.
Tversky, A. and Kahneman D. (1974). Judgment under uncertainty: Heuristics and biases, *Science* **185**(4157): 1124–1131.
Wakker, P. P. (2003). The data of Levy and Levy (2002) "Prospect theory: Much ado about nothing?" *Management Science* **49**(7): 979–981.

Section C. Stochastic dominance

Hanoch, G. and Levy, H. (1969). The efficiency analysis of choices involving risk, *Review of Economic Studies* **36**(3): 335–346.

Levy, H, (1973). Stochastic dominance, efficiency criteria, and efficient portfolios: The multi-period case, *American Economic Review* **63**(5): 986–994.

Levy, H and Paroush J. (1974). Multi-period stochastic dominance, *Management Science*, **21**(4): 428–435.

Section D. Risk aversion and static portfolio theory

Chopra, V. K. and Ziemba, W. T. (1993). The effect of errors in means, variances, and co-variances on optimal portfolio choice, *Journal of Portfolio Management* **19**: 6–11.

Kallberg, J. G. and Ziemba, W. T. (1983). Comparison of alternative utility functions in portfolio selection problems, *Management Science* **29**(11): 1257–1276.

Li, Y. and Ziemba, W. T. (1989). Characterizations of optimal portfolios by univariate and multivariate risk aversion, *Management Science* **35**(3): 259–269.

Li, Y. and Ziemba, W. T. (1993). Univariate and multivariate measures of risk aversion and risk premiums, *Annals of Operations Research* **45**: 265–296.

MacLean, L. C., Foster, M. E. and Ziemba, W. T. (2007). Covariance complexity and rates of return on assets, *Journal of Banking and Finance* **31**(11): 3503–3523.

Markowitz, H. M. (1952). Portfolio selection, *Journal of Finance* **7**: 77–91.

Markowitz, H. M. (1959). *Portfolio Selection: Efficient Diversification of Investments*. New York: Wiley and Sons.

Markowitz, H. M. (1987). *Mean-Variance Analysis in Portfolio Choice and Capital Markets*. Cambridge, MA: Basil Blackwell.

Pratt, J. W. (1964). Risk aversion in the small and in the large, *Econometrica* **32**(1–2): 122–136.

Rabin, M. and Thaler R. H. (2001). Anomalies: Risk aversion, *Journal of Economic Perspectives* **15**(1): 219–232.

Rubinstein, M. E. (1973). The fundamental theorem of parameter-preference security valuation, *Journal of Financial and Quantitative Analysis*, **8**: 61–70.

Ziemba, W. T. (1975). Choosing investment portfolios when the returns have stable distributions, in *Stochastic Optimization Models in Finance*, W. T. Ziemba and R. G. Vickson (eds.), San Diego: Academic Press, 243–266.

Ziemba, W. T., Parkan, C. and Brooks-Hill, R. (1974). Calculation of investment portfolios with risk free borrowing and lending, *Management Science* **21**(2): 209–222.

Section E. Risk measures

Föllmer, H. and Knispel, T. (2013). Convex risk measures: Basic facts, law-invariance and beyond, asymptotics for large portfolios, in *Handbook of the Fundamentals of Financial Decision Making*, L. C. MacLean and W. T. Ziemba (eds.), Singapore: World Scientific.

Geyer, A. and Ziemba, W. T. (2008). The innovest Austrian pension fund planning model InnoALM, *Operations Research* **56**(4): 797–810.

Jorion, P. (2006). *Value at Risk: The New Benchmark for Managing Financial Risk* (3rd edn.). New York: McGraw-Hill.

Krokhmal, P., Zabarankin, M. and Uryasev, S. (2011). Modeling and optimization of risk, *Surveys in Operations Research and Management Science* **16**(2): 49–66.

Rockafellar, R. T. and Ziemba W. T. (2000). Modified risk measures and acceptance sets, Working Paper.

Section F. Dynamic portfolio theory and asset allocation

Bahsoun, W., Evstigneev, I. V. and Taksar, M. I. (2013). Growth-optimal investments and numeraire of portfolios under transactions costs, in *Handbook of the Fundamentals of Financial Decision Making*, L. C. MacLean and W. T. Ziemba (eds.), Singapore: World Scientific.

Browne, S. (1999a). Beating a moving target: Optimal portfolio strategies for outperforming a stochastic benchmark, *Finance and Stochastics* **3**: 275–294.

Browne, S. (1999b). Reaching goals by a deadline: Digital options and continuous-time active portfolio management, *Advances in Applied Probability* **31**: 551–577.

Browne, S. (2000). Stochastic differential portfolio games, *Journal of Applied Probability* **37**(1): 126–147.

Campbell, J. Y., Chan Y. L. and Viceira, L. M. (2003). A multivariate model of strategic asset allocation, *Journal of Financial Economics* **67**: 41–80.

Davis, M. and Lleo, S. (2013). Fractional Kelly strategies in continuous time: Recent developments, in Handbook of the Fundamentals of Financial Decision Making, L. C. MacLean and W. T. Ziemba (eds.). Singapore: World Scientific.

Edirisinghe, C., Zhang, X. and Shyi, S.-C. (2013). DEA-based firm strengths and market efficiency in US and Japan, in *Handbook of the Fundamentals of Financial Decision Making*, L. C. MacLean and W. T. Ziemba (eds.). Singapore: World Scientific.

MacLean, L. C. and Ziemba, W. T. (2013). The Kelly strategy for investing: Risk and reward, in *Handbook of the Fundamentals of Financial Decision Making*, L. C. MacLean and W. T. Ziemba (eds.), Singapore: World Scientific.

Thorp E. O. and Mizusawa, S. (2013). Maximizing capital growth with black swan protection, in *Handbook of the Fundamentals of Financial Decision Making*, L. C. MacLean and W. T. Ziemba (eds.), Singapore: World Scientific.

(b) *Stochastic Optimization Models in Finance*, William T. Ziemba and Raymond G. Vickson (eds.), Editions 1 & 2 (1975, 2006)

PREFACE, Edition 1 (Academic Press, 1975)

There is no adequate book for an advanced course concerned with optimizing models of financial problems that involve uncertainty. The numerous texts and edited collections of articles related to quantitative business finance are largely concerned with deterministic models or stochastic models that are directly reducible to deterministic models. Our intention is that this present book of readings will partially fill this gap by providing a source that gives a reasonably thorough account of the mathematical theory and economic results relating to these problems. It is hoped that the volume can serve the dual role of text and research reference. The literature in this area is large and expanding rapidly. Hence to make the volume manageable we had to place severe constraints on our coverage. First and foremost we have only considered material relevant for optimizing models that explicitly involve uncertainty. As a result no material on statistical estimation procedures is included. Secondly, the concern is with the mathematical and economic theories involved and not with their application in practice and associated institutional aspects. However, our coverage does place emphasis on results and methods that can and have been utilized in the analysis of real financial problems. With some reluctance we also limited ourselves to models involving a single decision maker. Hence, material relating to gaming problems, market equilibrium, and other multiperson or multifirm problems is not included here. There is also very little material concerned with specific numerical algorithms or ad hoc solution approaches and that included is intended to be representative and not comprehensive.

The major criterion for inclusion of articles in the collection is that they present a significant methodological advance that is of lasting interest for teaching and research in finance. Since a major goal of the volume is to provide a source for students to "get quickly to the frontiers", preference was given to papers in areas where research is currently active. We have also tried to choose contributions that were well written and did not appear to have major gaps or errors in their presentation. Papers were also given lower priority if they have appeared in other books of readings or if similar material is available in such collections. This accounts for the very limited coverage of capital budget models. In several areas we felt it appropriate to provide new papers that summarize and extend existing results in the literature. Credit and blame for biases introduced in the selection of articles and their layout are due to WTZ.

The five parts of this work present material that is intended to be read in a sequential fashion part by part.

Part I is concerned with mathematical tools and expected utility theory. The treatment focuses on convexity and the Kuhn–Tucker conditions and the methods of dynamic programming. The next part is concerned with qualitative economic results, and particular attention is given to results relating to stochastic dominance, measures of risk aversion, and portfolio separation theorems. Part III is concerned with static models of portfolio selection. Particular attention is placed on the mean-variance and safety-first approaches and their extensions along with their relation to the expected utility approach. The questions of existence and diversifications of optimal portfolio policies and the effects of taxes on risk taking are also dealt with here. The fourth part is concerned with dynamic models that are in some sense reducible to static models. Part V is concerned with dynamic models that are most properly analyzed by dynamic methods. Particular attention is placed on models of portfolio revision, optimal capital accumulation, option strategies, and portfolio problems in continuous time.

Each part begins with an introduction that attempts to summarize and make cohesive the material that follows. This is followed by several articles that present major methodological advances in that area. At the end of each part there are numerous problems which form an integral part of the text and are subdivided into computational and review, and mind-expanding exercises. The computational and review exercises are intended to test the understanding of the preceding readings and how they relate to previous material. Some exercises present, hopefully, straightforward extensions, to new problems, of the methodological material in the readings. Other exercises fill gaps in the presentation of the reprinted articles. The mind-expanding exercises, on the other hand, are intended to traverse new problem areas whose analysis requires different techniques or non-straightforward extensions of the material in the reprinted articles. Many of these exercises are quite difficult, and some present unsolved problems and conjectures. We have starred all exercises whose solution is unknown or in doubt to us. Some mind-expanding exercises describe previously unpublished problems and solutions. They also serve to survey, to some extent, many important papers that could not be included because of space limitations. Indeed, many exercises present major results from one or more published papers. The sources from which such exercises were adapted are indicated in the "Exercise Source Notes" at the end of each exercise section. We have tried to present the exercises in such a way that the reader can obtain maximum benefit per unit input of time spent in their solution. In particular results are generally stated and the reader is asked to verify them. Hence, the student should be able to understand the major results and conclusions of a particular exercise even if he cannot solve all its parts.

This collection of articles and exercises has not undergone extensive classroom testing. However, one of us, William T. Ziemba (WTZ), has used some of the materials in courses at the University of British Columbia (in 1971) and at the University of California, Berkeley (in 1972). The typical students who would take a course based on this book are masters and doctoral level students in management science, operations research, and economics and doctoral level finance students. The ideal prerequisites consist of a course in elementary business finance using say Lusztig and Schwab (1973), Mao (1969), or Van Horne (1968), a course in nonlinear programming, using say Luenberger (1973) or Zangwill (1969), a course in probability theory using say Feller (1962) or Thomasion (1969), and a course in microeconomic theory using say Henderson and Quandt (1958) or Samuelson (1965). A course in intermediate capital theory using Fama and Miller (1972) or Mossin (1973) would also be of great value to the reader. Minimum prerequisites consist of a careful reading of Part I and the working of the accompanying computational and review exercises (perhaps supplemented by reading the first three chapters of Zangwill (1969) and Chapter Two of Arrow (1971), or by working the mind-expanding exercises in Part I); a calculus course using say Thomas (1953) or Allen (1971) and a course in intermediate probability theory using say Lippman (1971) or Hadley (1967). These minimum prerequisites should be adequate for the understanding of most of the articles in this volume if the reader has developed sufficient mathematical maturity. The book is intended for a two-semester course. It can also be used for a one-semester course related to static models (Parts I (1, 2), II, and III) or to dynamic models (Parts I (3), II (2), IV, and V).

Preface to the Second Edition (World Scientific, 2006)

Over the years we have been pleased that *Stochastic Optimization Models in Finance* has stood the test of time in being a path-breaking book concerned with optimizing models of financial problems that involve uncertainty. The book has been well known and respected for its excellent fundamental articles that are reprinted and the several new articles specifically written for the volume and additionally for its large collection of computational and review, and mind-expanding exercises. All of these appear in five separate parts with introductions that tie the articles in this book to the problems and these are further elaborated on the exercise source notes that discuss the literature further. Many of the mind-expanding exercises presaged important articles that later appeared in the financial economics literature. However, in recent years, the book has been hard for researchers, graduate students and professors to locate. Numerous publishers were interested in the problems as a separate book or a new fully reworked edition. We felt though that the book was a classic and should remain that way. Hence, we are extremely pleased that World Scientific is publishing this second edition with the only addition being this preface. The fundamentals in the 1975 Academic Press edition in Karl Shell's series of books on mathematical economics and econometrics are still fundamental, especially in static and dynamic portfolio theory, some 30 years later.

However, the world in 2006 in academic finance, mathematical finance, financial derivatives, financial econometrics, stochastic optimization, and multi-period stochastic programming and stochastic control optimization in finance and other areas has expanded enormously with much activity in leading trading and investment centers such as London, New York, Tokyo, Paris, Chicago, Boston, Sydney, Singapore and countless other places. New fields have evolved and many books and articles have been written in the large number of outstanding journals now publishing papers. These brief notes try to put *Stochastic Optimization Models in Finance* into 2006 in some perspective emphasizing areas WTZ is familiar with including some of his own work and how he is using or others could use the book in courses, seminars and workshops that deal with useful theory for real investment problems.

The 1975 edition was used by many students and faculty and helped evolve the then young field of optimization under uncertainty models of theory and economic results. Part I on mathematical tools focuses on expected utility theory, convexity and the Kuhn–Tucker conditions and dynamic programming. Each of these areas was well developed in 1975 however progress has continued in all three areas. Fishburn's comprehensive theory of subjective probabilities and expected utilities still provides an excellent introduction to utility theory. A notable subsequent area of expected utility theory is the prospect theory of Kahneman and Tversky (1979, 1984) and Tvernsky and Kahneman (1974), work for which Kahneman won the Nobel Prize in economics. They devised a utility theory to analyze the notion that individuals typically fear loss greater than they enjoy gains, that there is framing of decisions with different decisions made in identical situations except the way it is presented and that low probability events are typically overestimated and high probability events underestimated. These ideas are well accepted in financial engineering but not readily accepted in much of academic finance. These ideas are used in many places and some date from much earlier such as articles on the favorite-longshot bias related to the third Kahneman and Tversky area originally published in 1949 and 1957 reprinted in the racetrack efficiency studies volume of Hausch *et al.* (1994). The bias there is that high probability events have higher expected average returns and low probability events are greatly overestimated. Hausch *et al.* (1981) introduced the notion that biases might be exploitable in racetrack betting if you use probabilities from simple markets in complex markets. That paper and Hausch and Ziemba (1985) introduced Kelly betting into racetrack betting models. This area has grown immensely as well and a recent survey with updated results is in Hausch and Ziemba (2008). Tompkins *et al.* (2008) show that biases are similar in the S&P500 and the FTSE100 stock indices as well. The two Mangasarian papers on pseudo-convex and composite functions remain classics to this day and are constantly used in portfolio theory by those who know about them. Dynamic programming remains an active field and it is frequently used in economic and financial studies. My paper is still a useful introduction to the theory and concepts. Campbell and Viceira (2002) is a recent example and shows that current research in continuous time dynamic programming focuses on computational strategies and qualitative economic results.

Part II discusses stochastic dominance, measures of risk aversion and portfolio separation theorems. The 1969 Hanoch–Levy stochastic dominance paper is still the starting point in this area and takes graduate students to a good understanding of when distribution X is preferred to distribution Y. Besides having the basic first and second order stochastic dominance results, it contains the single crossing result that if distributions cross only once then the one with the higher mean has higher expected utility for all concave risk averse investors. This result shows when expected utility theory and mean variance analysis coincide; see also the Samuelson and Ohlson papers in part III on this. In WTZ's lectures he also uses Rothschild and Stiglitz (1970) which shows that the notion of using mean preserving spreads to show that more weight in the tails is equivalent to second order stochastic dominance results. These economic results date back to mathematical treatments of Blackwell and Girchik (1954) and Hardy *et al.* (1934); and Diamond and Stiglitz (1974) who show that concave in parameters investors bet less with increasing risk. Brumelle and Vickson (written for this book) go deeply into the mathematics of these concepts. The 1964 Pratt paper is still the fundamental one in risk aversion. It suggests good utility functions for use by individuals and organizations with decreasing absolute risk aversion, concavity and monotonicity. These include the double exponential (see Chapter 1 of Ziemba, 2003) for a worked out example) and log and negative power (see Bell, 1995, for the case of linear plus exponential).

Less well known is Rubinstein's risk aversion measure which has optimality in financial equilibrium (Rubinstein, 1976) and portfolio theory (Kallberg and Ziemba, 1983). However, in practice, the

Arrow–Pratt measure, as it is known, is more useful since it can be estimated in various ways and used in static as well as dynamic models such as Cariño *et al.* (1994, 1998b), Cariño and Ziemba (1998a) and Geyer *et al.* (2005). This area also led to the modern notion of risk measures, which were developed using an Arrow-like axiomatic system in Artzner *et al.* (1999). Subsequent work such as in Rockafellar and Ziemba (2000) and especially in Föllmer and Scheid (2002a, 2002b) rationalized the convex risk measures used in the stochastic programming literature starting with Kusy and Ziemba (1986). These risk measures are theoretical improvements on the value at risk (VaR). With VaR, one presupposes a cutoff loss level and a confidence level such that one will not lose more than this amount with that probability. Hence, it is like a chance-constraint and has the same drawbacks. For example, the penalty is independent of the loss. Rockafellar and Uryasev (2000) show that the linear in the penalty approximation of VaR, called CVar, can be computed endogenously and exogenously via a linear program. Our exercise ME-26 shows this for the much simpler exogenous case, where the constraint confidence level is specified in advance.

The Lintner and Vickson (written for this book) papers in section 3 of part II discuss extensions of Tobin's 1958 separation theorem that evolves when there is, as Tobin suggested, a risk-free asset. So does Ziemba's stable distribution paper in part III that further extends the idea to fat-tailed stable distributions and Ziemba *et al.* (1974) which specifically shows how to compute the two parts of the separation in Tobin's normal distribution world: the mutual fund (i.e., market index) that is independent of the investor's assumed to be concave utility function and the optimal balance of cash and this mutual fund for any given utility function. The first problem is deterministic in n-variables and solved as a linear complementary or quadratic programming problem. The second problem is stochastic but has only one variable, the percent cash. Ross (1976) approaches the analysis in a more general way than the normal, stable or other distributional form and obtains theoretical conditions for separation but it is not clear how to find the separated portfolios.

Part III deals with static portfolio selection models and begins with papers by Samuelson and Ohlson (written for this book) that show when mean-variance analysis is optimal in cases other than normal distribution and quadratic utility but with special distributions that converge properly. Pyle and Turnovsky's analysis of safety first *à la* Roy's 1952 *Econometrica* papers that was a close alternative to Markowitz's (1952) famous portfolio theory paper that ushered in modern investment management and gave Markowitz the Nobel prize in economics in 1990. This area presages the CVar literature which has become very extensive since 2000 with contributions including the *Journal of Banking and Finance* special issue, see Krokhmal *et al.* (2006) and the volume edited by Szego (2004). Davis and Norman (1990) and Davis, Panas and Zariphopoulou (1993) present portfolio theory with transaction costs. Duffie and Pan (1997) and Jorion (2006) survey the values of risk literature. Ziemba's stable distribution paper uses generalized concave mathematical programming ideas to generalize normal distribution Markowitz and Tobin portfolio theory to the infinite variance fat-tailed stable distribution case. Applications of stable modeling are still less common in the literature but many real asset prices such as Japanese golf course prices fit such distributions; see Stone and Ziemba (1993).

Popular modern investment texts such as Brealey and Myers (2006) and Bodie *et al.* (2005) generally present investment theory in its pure form. But in reality, taxes and transaction costs are crucial much of the time. The Stiglitz and Naslund papers in section 3 of part III were early fundamental contributions to the theory of the effects of taxes on risk taking behavior. This area is a rich one with many subsequent practical studies such as the volumes edited for the NBER by James Poterba, theoretical studies by George Constantinides and Mark Davis and others.

Perhaps the greatest change in applied research since the first edition of *Stochastic Optimization Models in Finance* in 1975 is the emphasis and computations concerning dynamic models with uncertainty. We now have publicly available codes to solve multi-period stochastic programming models with millions of variables and scenarios. In fact 10 such systems are described in Wallace and Ziemba (2005).

Parts IV and V of the volume discuss dynamic models with uncertainty taken into account in the decision making process. Some models can be reduced to or analyzed as static models in some way and the papers by Wilson, Fama and Hakansson discuss three such ways to do this. Wilson's model has a single decision point. Fama shows the notion that many dynamic stochastic models are equivalent to a static model where the future period's random variables have been expected out and the future period's decision variables have been optimized out. This notion has been used in stochastic programming literature since the early paper of Dantzig (1955) and is standard in the current theoretical literature, see e.g., Birge and Louveaux (1997) or Wets and Ziemba (1999). The results show that concavity is preserved over maximization and expectation but not over strict concavity without additional assumptions, see Ziemba (1974, 1977) on this latter point.

Mossin (1968) showed that for essentially unconstrained dynamic investment problems with power utility functions that the optimal policy was myopic if the asset returns were independent period by period. Hakansson's paper (1971) showed that if the objective function was logarithmic, then an optimal myopic policy existed for general dependent assets. This paper and those by Breiman and Thorp in section 4 of part V concern the extremely important but little used (except by some rather talented people discussed below) Kelly (1956) capital growth theory.

Section V concerns dynamic models and begins with Vickson's intuitive discussion of the Itô calculus for stochastic differential equations and stochastic optimal control used in continuous time finance. The only real continuous time paper in the volume is Merton's in section 4. Two major areas have evolved out of continuous time finance whose father is Robert C. Merton who won the Nobel Prize in economics in 1997 for his work related to the Black–Scholes (1973) and Merton (1973) option pricing model. The area has exploded with thousands of articles and hundreds of books on option pricing models and applications published since these fundamental contributions were made. Our book just touches the surface of such work so we refer readers to such option pricing and derivative security books as Rubinstein (1998), Duffie (2001), Shreve (2004), Hull (2006), and Wilmott (2006). In this area, the continuous time modeling is crucial to the option pricing. One area of use is in hedge fund mispricing that is buy A and sell A', a close substitute but which is more expensive. Then wait in this risk arbitrage until the prices converge within a transactions cost band. Most such modeling is confidential and kept secret but one such application to the 1990 Nikkei put warrant market is described in Shaw *et al.* (1995).

The other area which is well explained in Merton's (1992) book is the whole notion of using continuous time finance in a vast number of other applications. One to asset-liability management which extends the Tobin (1958) separation theorem to multiple aggregated assets as Merton did in his book is Rudolf and Ziemba (2004). There are a group of aggregated mutual funds such that investment by all concave risk averse investors is optimal across just these mutual funds with the weights depending on the specific utility function. Merton shows this for the assets-only case and Rudolf–Ziemba (2004) add the liabilities mutual fund. The hedge fund D. E. Shaw uses the Rudolf–Ziemba (2004) model.

These are aggregated assets or funds and it is optimal for all concave risk investors to choose among them. Then, once the investor and his utility function is specified optimal portfolio weights in the funds may be determined. One of the drawbacks of continuous time models is their great sensitivity to parameter uncertainly. So in ALM stochastic programming models such as those in Ziemba and Mulvey (1998), Wallace and Ziemba (2005) and Zenios and Ziemba (2006, 2007) are generally preferred by pensions, insurance companies, wealthy individuals and hedge funds; see Ziemba (2003).

One advantage of these scenario based models is that the parameters are not assumed to be known but are scenario dependent, that is, uncertain. Also they have discrete portfolio revision periods as are used in most investment processes.

Drèze and Modigliani (1972) present a two period model of Irving Fisher's theory of savings under uncertainty where the main issues center on the tradeoff of current versus future consumption. This is modeled so that risk aversion affects this choice and the resulting portfolio choices. The economic results obtained would generalize to what one might obtain in a multi-period version which current technology could now easily analyze.

Bradley and Crane present a multistage decision tree model for bond portfolio management. A novel feature was its ability to trace the bond movements from interest rate changes over time. This model is one of dynamic programming rather than stochastic programming hence its size grows faster than the latter. Kusy and Ziemba (1986) compare their stochastic programming model from the Vancouver Savings Credit Union with that of Bradley–Crane (1972) and argue for the SP model on computational and performance grounds. Both of these models are now easily solved with current technology as in Wallace and Ziemba (2005). The Bradley and Crane model ushered in a whole literature in bond portfolio management; see for example the papers by Zenios, and Bertocchi and Dupacova in Zenios and Ziemba (2006, 2007) for the current state of this literature which has moved more to the SP model approach using complex bond pricing which Bradley and Crane initiated in this paper. They Kusy and Ziemba approach was the first of many aggregated ALM models which include the Russell Yasuda model, see Cariño *et al.* (1994, 1998a, 1998b) and the Siemens Austria pension fund model, see Geyer *et al.* (2005) and papers in Ziemba and Mulvey (1998), Wallace and Ziemba (2005) and the Zenios and Ziemba ALM Handbook (2006, 2007).

Section 2 of part V deals with models of optimal capital accumulation and portfolio selection. Neave presents conditions for a consumer's multi-period utility function to exhibit both decreasing absolute and increasing relative risk aversion. He shows that these properties are preserved through maximization and expectation operations over time. Although some generalizations are possible, Neave essentially solves this problem.

Samuelson and Merton in a pair of companion articles in 1969 devised the discrete time and continuous time dynamic portfolio consumption-investment models, respectively, which are very active in current research. Merton's paper and his 1971 paper in section 2 of part V are highly related to current continuous time models such as those descried in his book (Merton, 1992) and in the strategic asset allocation work of Brennan and Schwartz (1997, 1998) and Campbell and Viceira (2002), as well as the Black and Scholes (1973) and Merton (1973) option pricing models. For option pricing, the continuous time model is essential but for practical asset-liability modelling the discrete time multi-period stochastic programming models are more practical as they can bring to the model more of the real constraints and preferences through targets and are less sensitive to parameter errors then the continuous time models whose optimal weights are moved dramatically in an instant with the arrival of new information.

Hakansson's 1970 paper along with Breiman's 1960 and Thorp's 1971 papers concern the Kelly criterion as it is called in the gambling literature or the capital growth criterion in the finance and economics literature. See also Williams (1936) and Latane (1959) for early related treatments of this subject. Hakansson's 1971 paper in part IV showed, that with log utility, one has optimal myopic behavior in dynamic investment/consumption models. In this paper, Hakansson obtains closed form optimal consumption, investment and borrowing strategies for constant relative or absolute Arrow–Pratt risk aversion indices which includes various power, log and exponential utility functions. Breiman and in his more detailed paper Breiman (1961) show the powerful long run properties of log utility investing. These include the fact that the log investor will, as time increases without limit, have more wealth, in fact arbitrarily more wealth, than any other investor as long as the strategies differ infinitely often. Moreover, the log investor will achieve goals sufficiently large faster than any other such investor. Thorp further expands the theory but more importantly uses it in sports betting and in hedge fund risk arbitrage in the financial markets such as in warrant trading. He also points out that Breiman's results can be generalized and the papers of Algoet and Cover (1988), Thorp (2006) and MacLean and Ziemba (2006) do that and survey other aspects of the theory and practice of log betting. Early on MacLean and I worked on the marriage of growth and security through fractional Kelly strategies; see e.g., MacLean *et al.* (1992). For these, essentially negative power utility functions, growth is less but so is wealth variability.

Since the risk aversion of log is one divided by wealth or essentially zero, log is an exceedingly risky utility function in the short run. And this is doubly so if there are parameter errors since the errors in the mean which normally are 20:2:1 as important as those of the variances and covariances become 100:2:1 with low risk aversion; see Chopra and Ziemba (1993) which updated and added risk aversion to the earlier Kallberg and Ziemba (1981, 1984) studies. Hence, over betting is very dangerous with log. Markowitz in a private communication with me proved the result that MacLean *et al.* (1992) saw empirically that betting double the Kelly fraction (which maximizes the long run growth rate) actually makes the growth rate zero plus the risk-free rate; see Ziemba (2003), for more discussion and the proof. Indeed, this is one explanation for part of the demise of Long Term Capital Management in 1998 from over betting. Thorp and I are proponents of the Kelly and fractional Kelly approach and observe that many of the world's greatest investors like Warren Buffett, John Maynard Keynes, Bill Benter in horseracing in Hong Kong and Thorp himself used such strategies. I personally consulted for six such individuals who turned zero into hundreds of millions or even billions (in the case of Jim Simons of Renaissance who made 1.4 billion just in 2005). Ziemba (2005) and MacLean and Ziemba (2006) study many of these investors and Thorp (2006) discusses his use of the Kelly approach and that of Buffett, who acts as if he was a full Kelly bettor.

Samuelson, see his article in part V, however, is not a log utility supporter. His objections are recorded in the conclusion to his article. He argues that maximizing the geometric mean rather than the arithmetic mean maximizes expected utility only for log utility. Indeed we know that log is the most risky utility function one should ever consider in the short run. Donald Hausch and I did a simulation, see Ziemba and Hausch (1986) reproduced in MacLean and Ziemba (2006) to understand this better. We take an investor with $1,000 and who bets with log and half Kelly $(-w^{-1})$ 700 times with five possible wagers with probability of winning 0.19 to 0.57 corresponding to $1-1, 2-1, \ldots, 5-1$ odds with a 14% expected value advantage. The bets are independent. There are 1,000 trials. In 166 of the 1,000 trials, the final wealth for log is greater than 100 times the initial $1,000. With half Kelly it is only once this large. But half Kelly provides higher probability of being ahead etc. So there is a growth-security trade-off. However, it is possible to make 700 independent bets all with a 14% advantage and still lose 98% of ones wealth. Half Kelly is not much better. You can still lose 86% of your initial wealth. So the conclusion is that log is short term risky and long term wins you the most money. Once compromise, see MacLean *et al.* (2004) is to choose at discrete internals the fractional Kelly that would keep you above a wealth path with high probability. This we have just implemented in a hedge fund but with a convex penalty for falling below the path. Log is certainly the most interesting and controversial utility function for investment. It is rarely taught. Despite their original publishing dates, the papers by Breiman, Hakannson, Samuelson and Thorp in the volume well represent a very good beginning for students of this area.

Section 3 of part IV has various models of option strategy prior to Black–Scholes (1973) and Merton (1973). Pye and Taylor present specific models to value call options on bonds and stocks. Kalymon formulates a bond. refunding problem where future interest rates are Markovian. He can then determine policies that minimize expected total discounted costs. Finally, Pye shows that dollar cost averaging is a minimax strategy rather than an expected utility maximizing strategy for any strictly concave utility function.

References to subsequent papers and books not appearing in this volume that may be useful in courses and for further study using this volume follow.

William T. Ziemba

Vancouver, June 2006

References

Algeot, P. and Cover, T. (1988). Asymptotic optimality and asymptotic equipartition properties of log-optimum investment. *Annals of probability* **16**, 876–898.

Allen, R. G. D. (1971), *Mathematical Analysis for Economists*. New York: Macmillan.

Arrow, K. J. (1974). "The Use of Unbounded Utility Functions in Expected-Utility Maximization: Response." *The Quarterly Journal of Economics*, **88**, 136–138.

Artzner, P., Delbaen, F., Eber, J.-M. and Heath, D. (1999). Coherent measures of risk, *Mathematical Finance* **9**: 203–227.

Bell, D. (1995). Risk, return and utility, *Management Science* **41**: 23–30.

Birge, J. and Louveaux, F. (1977). *Stochastic Programming*. Berlin: Springer.

Black, F. and Scholes, M. S. (1973). The pricing of options and corporate liabilities, *Journal of Political Economy* **81**: 637–654.

Blackwell, D. and Girchik, M. A. (1954). *Theory of Games and Statistical Decisions*, New York: Wiley.

Bodie, Z., Kane, A. and Marcus, A. J. (2005). *Investments* (6th edn.). Boston: Irwin McGraw.

Bradley, Stephen P. and Crane, Dwight B. (1972). *Management Science* **19**, 139–151.

Brealey, R. A. and Myers, S. (2006). *Principles of Corporate Finance*. New York: McGraw Hill.

Breiman, L. (1960). Investment policies for expanding business in a long-run sense. *Naval Research Logistics Quarterly* **7**, 647–651.

Breiman, L. (1961). Optimal gambling systems for favorable games. *Symp. Probability and Statist. 4th, Berkeley, 1961*, **1**, 65–78.

Brennan, M. J., Schwartz, E.S. and Lagnado, R. (1997). Strategic asset allocation. *Journal of Economic Dynamics and Control* **21**, 1377–1403.

Brennan, M. J. and Schwartz, E.S. (1998). Time Invariant Portfolio Insurance Strategies, *The Journal of Finance* **43**(2), 283–300.

Campbell, J. Y. and Viceira, L. (2002). *Strategic Asset Allocation.* Oxford: Oxford University Press.

Cariño, D. *et al.* (1994). The Russell–Yasuda Kasai model: An asset/liability model for a Japanese insurance company using multistage stochastic programming, *INTERFACES* (**January–February**) (Edelman Prize issue): 29–49.

Cariño, D., Myers, D. and Ziemba, W. T. (1998b). Concepts, technical issues and uses of the Russell–Yasuda Kasai financial planning model, *Operations Research* **46**(4): 450–462.

Cariño, D. and Ziemba, W. T. (1998a). Formulation of the Russell–Yasuda Kasai financial planning model, *Operations Research*, **46**(4): 433–449.

Chopra, V. and W. Ziemba (1993). The effect of errors in the mean. variance, and covariance estimates on optimal portfolio choice. *Journal of Portfolio Management*, Winter, 6–11.

Dantzig, G. B. (1955). Linear programming under uncertainty, *Management Science* **1**(3): 197–206.

Davis, M. H. A. and Norman, A. R. (1990). Portfolio selection with transaction costs, *Math of Operations Research* **15**: 676–713.

Davis, M. H. A., Panas, V. G. and Zariphopoulou, T. (1993). European option pricing with transaction costs, *SIAM Journal of Control and Optimization* **31**: 470–493.

Diamond, P. and Stiglitz, J. E. (1974). Increases in risk and in risk aversion, *Journal of Economic Theory* **8**: 337–350.

Drèze, Jacques H. and Modigliani, Franco (1972). *Journal of Economic Theory* **5**, 308–335.

Duffie, D. (2001). *Dynamic Asset Pricing Theory* (3rd edn.). Princeton: Princeton University Press.

Duffie, D. and Pan, J. (1997). An overview of value at risk, *Journal of Derivatives* (Spring): 7–49.

Edward O. Thorp (1971). Business and economics statistics section. *Proceedings of the American Statistical Association*, 215–224.

Fama, E. F., and Miller, M. H. (1972). *The Theory of Finance.* New York: Holt.

Feller, W. (1962). *An Introduction to Probability Theory and its Applications*, Vol. I. New York: Wiley.

Föllmer, H. and Scheid, A. (2002a). Convex measures of risk and trading constraints, *Finance and Statistics* **6**(4): 429–447.

Föllmer, H. and Scheid, A. (2002b). *Stochastic Finance: An Introduction in Discrete Time*. Berlin: deGruyter.

Geyer, A., Herold, W., Kontriner, K. and Ziemba, W. T. (2005). The innovest Austrian pension fund planning model innoALM, Working Paper, Sauder School of Business, UBC.

Hadley, G. (1967). *Introduction to Probability and Statistical Decision Theory*. San Francisco, California: Holden-Day.

Hakansson, N. H. (1970). Optimal investment and consumption strategies under risk for a class of utility functions. *Econometrica* **38**(5), 587–607.

Hakansson N. H. (1971). *The Journal of Business of the University of Chicago* **44**, 324–334.

Hardy, G. H., Littlewood, J. E. and Polya, G. (1934). *Inequalities*. Cambridge: Cambridge University Press.

Hausch, D. B. and Ziemba, W. T. (1985). Transactions costs, entries and extent of inefficiencies in a racetrack betting model, *Management Science* **XXXI**: 381–394.

Hausch, D. B. and Ziemba, W. T. (eds.) (2008). *Handbook of Sports and Lottery Investments*. Amsterdam: Elsevier.

Hausch, D. B., Lo, V. and Ziemba, W. T. (eds.) (1994). *The Efficiency of Racetrack Betting Markets*. San Diego: Academic Press.

Hausch, D.B., Ziemba, W. T. and Rubinstein, M. (1981). Efficiency of the Market for Racetrack Betting, *Management Science* **XXVII**: 1435–1452.

Henderson, J. M., and Quandt, R. E. (1958). *Microeconomic Theory*. New York: McGraw-Hill.

Hull, J. (2006). *Options, Futures and other Derivatives* (6th Edn.). Upper Saddle River: Prentice-Hall.

Jorion, P. (2006). *Value-at-Risk: The Benchmark for Controlling Market Risk* (2nd Edn.). New York: McGraw-Hill.

Kahneman, D. and Tversky, A. (1979). Prospect theory: An analysis of decisions under risk, *Econometrica* **47**(2): 263–291.

Kallberg, J. G., and Ziemba, W. T. (1981). Remarks on optimal portfolio selection. *Methods of Operations Research* **44**, 507–520.

Kallberg, J. G. and Ziemba, W. T. (1983). Comparison of alternative utility functions in portfolio selection problems, *Management Science* **XXIX**: 1257–1276.

Kallberg, J. G., and Ziemba, W. T. (1984). Mis-specification in portfolio selection problems, in *Risk and capital*, Bamberg and Spreemann (eds.). Springer-Verlag, 74–87.

Kelly, J. (1956). A new interpretation of information rate, *Bell System Technology Journal* **35**: 917–926.

Krokhmal, P., Rockafellar, R. T. and Uryasev, S. (2006). Special issue on risk management and optimization in finance, *Journal of Banking and Finance* **30**(2): 743–778.

Kusy, M. I. and Ziemba, W. T. (1986). A bank asset and liability management model, *Operations Research* **XXXIV**: 356–376.

Latané, H. A. (1959). Criteria for choice among risky ventures. *JPE* **67**, 144–155.

Lippman, S. A. (1971). *Elements of Probability and Statistics*. New York: Holt.

Luenberger, D. E. (1973). *Introduction to Linear and Nonlinear Programming*. Reading Massachusetts: Addison-Wesley.

Lusztig, P. A., and Schwab, B. (1973). *Managerial Finance in a Canadian Setting*. New York: Holt.

MacLean, L. C., Ziemba, W. T. and Blazenko, G. (1992). Growth versus security in dynamic investment analysis, *Management Science* **38**(November, Special Issue on Financial Modelling): 1562–1585.

MacLean, L. and Ziemba, W. T. (2006). Capital Growth: Theory and Practice, in *Handbook of Asset and Liability Management*, S. Zenios and W. T. Ziemba (eds.). Amsterdam: Elsevier Science.

MacLean, L., Ziemba, W. T., Zhao, Y., and Sangree, R. (2004). Capital growth with security. *Journal of Economic Dynamics and Control* **28**(5), 937–954.

Mao, J. C. T. (1969). *Quantitative Analysis of Financial Decisions*. New York: Macmillan.

Markowitz, H. M. (1952). Portfolio selection, *Journal of Finance* **7**(1): 77–91.

Merton, R. C. (1973). The theory of rational option pricing, *Bell Journal of Economics and Management* **4**: 141–183.

Merton, R. C. (1992). *Continuous Time Finance* (2nd Edn.). Malden Blackwell Publishers, Inc.

Mossin, J. (1968). Optimal multiperiod portfolio policies, *Journal of Business* **41**(2): 215–229.

Mossin, J. (1973). *Theory of Financial Markets*. Englewood Cliffs, New Jersey: Prentice Hall.

Rockafellar, R. T. and Uryasev, S. (2000). Optimization of conditional value-at-risk, *Journal of Risk* **2**: 21–41.

Rockafellar, R. T. and Ziemba, W. T. (2000). Axiomatic convex risk measures, Technical Report, University of Washington.

Ross, S. A. (1978). Mutual fund separation in financial theory — the separating distributions, *Journal of Economic Theory* **17**: 254–286.

Rothschild, M. and Stiglitz, J. E. (1970). Increasing risk I: A definition, *Journal of Economic Theory* **2**: 225–243.

Roy, A. D. (1952). Safety-first and the holding of assets, *Econometrica* **20**(July): 431–449.

Rubinstein, M. (1976). The valuation of uncertain income streams and the pricing of options, *Bell Journal of Economics* **7**: 407–425.

Rubinstein, M. (1998). *Derivatives: A Power Point Picture Book, Volume 1: Futures, Options and Dynamic Strategies*, self published. University of California: Haas School of Business.

Rudolf, M. and Ziemba, W. T. (2004). Intertemporal asset-liability management, *Journal of Economic Dynamics and Control* **28**(4): 975–990.

Samuelson, P. A. (1965). *Foundations of Economic Analysis*. New York: Atheneum.

Shaw, J., Thorp, E. O. and Ziemba, W. T. (1995). Convergence to efficiency of the Nikkei put warrant market of 1989–90, *Applied Mathematical Finance* **2**: 243–271.

Shreve, S. E. (2004). *Stochastic Calculus for Finance, Volume II: Continuous Time Models*. Berlin: Springer-Verlag.

Stone, D. and Ziemba, W. T. (1993). Land and stock prices in Japan, *Journal of Economic Perspectives* **7**(3): 149–165.

Szego, G. (2004). *Risk Measures for the 21st Century*. New York: Wiley.

Thomas, G. B. Jr. (1953). *Calculus*. Reading, Massachusetts: Addison-Wesley.

Thomasion, A. J. (1969). *The Structure of Probability Theory with Applications*. New York: McGraw-Hill.

Thorp, E. (2006). The Kelly Criterion in Blackjack, Sports Betting and the Stock Market, in *Handbook of Asset and Liability Management*, S. Zenios and W. T. Ziemba (eds.). Amsterdam: Elsevier Science.

Tobin, J. (1958). Liquidity preference as behavior towards risk, *Review of Economic Studies* **26**(February): 65–86.

Tompkins, R. G., Ziemba, W. T. and Hodges, S. D. (2008). The favorite-longshot bias in S&P500 and FSTE 100 index futures options: The return to bets and the cost of insurance, in *Handbook of Sports and Lottery Markets*, D. B. Hausch and W. T. Ziemba (eds.). Amsterdam: North-Holland, 161–180.

Van Home, J. C. (1968). *Financial Management and Policy*. Englewood Cliffs, New Jersey: Prentice Hall.

Wallace, S. W. and Ziemba, W. T. (eds.) (2005). *Applications of Stochastic Programming*, SIAM — Mathematical Programming Series on Optimization, Philadelphia.

Wets, R. J. B. and Ziemba, W. T. (eds.) (1999). *Stochastic Programming — State of the Art 1998*, (main lectures VIII International Conference on Stochastic Programming). Baltzer Science Publishers BV (Special Issue Annals of Operations Research).

Williams, J. B. (1936). Speculation and the carryover, *Quarterly Journal of Economics* **50**(May): 436–455.

Wilmott, P. (2006). *Paul Wilmott on Quantitative Finance*, Vols. 1–3, (2nd Edn.). Hoboken: Wiley.

Zangwill, W. I. (1969). *Nonlinear Programming: A Unified Approach.* Englewood Cliffs, New Jersey: Prentice Hall.

Ziemba, W. T. (1974). Note on the behavior of a firm subject to stochastic regulatory review, *Bell Journal of Economics and Management Sciences* **5**(2): 710–712.

Ziemba, W. T. (1977). Multiperiod consumption–investment decisions: further comments, *American Economic Review* **LXVII**: 766–767.

Ziemba, W. T. (2005). The symmetric downside-risk Sharpe ratio and the evaluation of great investors and speculators. *Journal of Portfolio Management*, Fall, 108–122.

Ziemba, W. T., and Hausch, D. B. (1986). Betting at the Racetrack. Dr. Z Investments, Inc., San Luis Obispo, Ca.

Ziemba, W. T., Parkan, C. and Brooks-Hill, F. J. (1974). Calculation of investment portfolios with risk free borrowing and lending, *Management Science* **XXI**: 209–222.

Ziemba, W. T. and Mulvey, J. M. (eds.) (1998). *Asset and Liability Management from a Global Perspective.* Cambridge: Cambridge University Press.

Ziemba, W. T. (2003). *The Stochastic Programming Approach to Asset Liability and Wealth Management.* Charlottesville, VA: AIMR.

Zenios, S. A. and Ziemba, W. T. (eds.) (2006, 2007). *Handbook of Asset and Liability Modeling*, two volumes 1 on theory and methodology and 2 on applications and case studies. Amsterdam: North Holland.

SECTION A: ARBITRAGE
AND ASSET PRICING

The theme of this book is financial decision making. The decisions are the amount of investment capital to allocate to various opportunities in a financial market. The opportunity set can be very complex, with sets of equities, bonds, commodities, derivatives, futures, and currencies changing stochastically and dynamically over time. To consider decisions in a complex market it is necessary to impose structure. In the abstract, the assets and, the participants buying and selling them, are parts of a system with underlying economic states. The system's dynamics and the factors defining the states in the system have been studied extensively in finance and economics. The dynamics of the market and the behavior of participants determine the trading prices of the various assets in the opportunity set.

A simplifying assumption is that the financial market is perfectly competitive. There are conditions which must be present for a perfectly competitive market structure to exist. There must be many participants in the market, none of which is large enough to affect prices. Individuals should be able to buy and sell without restriction. All participants in the market have complete information about prices. In the competitive market, investors are price takers. These assumptions are strong, and in real financial markets they are not exactly satisfied. However, with the assumed structure an idealized market can be characterized and that provides a standard by which existing practice can be measured. As well, deviations from the idealized market can give indications of which assumptions are violated.

If investors are price takers, then a fundamental component of financial decision making is asset pricing. A common approach to asset pricing is to derive equilibrium prices for assets in a competitive market. This can be achieved with a model mapping the abstract states defined by a probability space into prices of assets such as equities and bonds. The Capital Asset Pricing Model (CAPM) developed independently by Sharpe (1964), Lintner (1965), Mossin (1966) and Treynor (1961, 1962) is a standard for pricing risky assets. Some clarification was provided by Fama (1968). The model proposes that the expected excess return of a risky asset over a riskless asset is proportional to the expected excess return of the market over the riskless asset. It is assumed that investor preferences are expressed in terms of means and variances/covariances. In this setting the financial market is in competitive equilibrium. Consistent with this structure, the optimal investment decisions are determined from the mean-variance approach developed by Markowitz (1952, 1959). The CAPM is the theoretical basis for much of the sizable index fund business. Dimension Fund Advisors alone manages more than $250 billion, most of which is passive.

The CAPM model has a single explanatory variable, the market portfolio, in a simple linear regression. This model has been extended to include other market variables in a multivariate linear regression. For example, following Rosenberg (1974), Rosenberg *et al.* (1985), Fama and French (1992) have added two explanatory variables: (i) small minus large capitalization; and (ii) high minus low book to market ratio.

The equilibrium pricing in the CAPM type models assumes that no arbitrage opportunities exist. An arbitrage is a transaction that involves no negative cash flow at any probabilistic or temporal state and a positive cash flow in at least one state; in simple terms, it is the possibility of a risk-free profit at zero cost. The Arbitrage Pricing Theory (APT) for asset pricing following from an assumption of no arbitrage was developed by Ross (1976). This theory defines the expected returns on assets with a linear factor model. The theory linking arbitrage to the factor model are presented in the paper "The Arbitrage Theory of Capital Asset Pricing". The Ross argument considers a well-diversified portfolio of risky assets which uses no wealth (free lunch). The portfolio is essentially independent of noise. If the portfolio has no risk, then the random return is certain and to avoid disequilibrium the certain return must be zero. This no arbitrage condition implies that the returns on the assets are defined by a linear relation to a set of common random factors with zero expectation. This type of equilibrium arbitrage argument follows the famous Modigliani and Miller paper (1958) and is part of the reasoning in the Black–Scholes option pricing (1973) model.

In the CAPM and APT models, the "no arbitrage" condition is necessary. If the market setting is a hyperfinite continuum of assets, then "no arbitrage" is sufficient for both CAPM and APT. It is required in that setting that asset returns satisfy a bounded variation assumption. (See Kahn and Sun, 1997).

There are a number of differences between the CAPM and APT theories. The most significant distinction is the "factors". In CAPM the factors/independent variables are manifest market variables (e.g., market index). With APT the factors are intrinsic (not manifest) variables, whose existence follows from diversification and no arbitrage. It is not required that the APT factors have clear definitions as entities. The APT factors are structural, without implied causation. That is, CAPM: factors → returns; APT: factors ↔ returns. So the factor model in APT is really a distributional condition on prices following from no arbitrage. The essence of arbitrage is captured in Ross' theory.

There are no assumptions in APT about the distribution of noise. However, the use of the factor model in empirical work on pricing does use algorithms which sometime assume normality of the factors and returns. The statistical estimation would also suggest definitions/entities for the intrinsic factors, which could further link the CAPM and APT models. Factor models have been used in practice by many analysts (see Jacobs and Levy (1988), Ziemba and

Schwartz (1991), and Schwartz and Ziemba (2000)). Companies such as BARRA lease these models.

The APT does not assume the existence of a competitive equilibrium. Disequilibrium can exist in the theory, but it is assumed that in aggregate the returns are uniformly bounded.

The no arbitrage assumption is a natural condition to expect of a stable financial market. The existence of arbitrage free prices for assets is linked to the probability measure on which the stochastic process of prices is defined. The Fundamental Theorem of Asset Pricing states that.

If $P = \{P_t, t \geq 0\}$ are asset prices in a complete financial market, then the following statements are equivalent:

(i) P does not allow for arbitrage.
(ii) There exists a probability measure which is equivalent to the original underlying measure and the price process is a martingale under the new measure.

A martingale is a stochastic process where the conditional expected value for the next period equals the current observed value, and does not depend on the history of the process. So a martingale is a model for a fair process and it is not surprising that the fairness of no arbitrage can be characterized by a martingale measure. Indeed the Ross (1976) argument establishes the link between arbitrage and a martingale measure using the famous Hahn–Banach theorem. The assumptions used by Ross on the underlying measure were somewhat limiting. In the case of an infinite probability space, the Ross result only applies to the sup norm topology. For finite dimensional space, it is not clear that the martingale measure is actually equivalent.

These limitations were considered by Harrison and Kreps (1979) and Harrison and Pliska (1981). They extended the Fundamental Theorem of Asset Pricing in several ways:

(i) If the price process is defined on a finite, filtered, probability space, then the market contains no arbitrage possibilities if and only if there is an equivalent martingale measure.

(ii) If the price process is defined on a continuous probability space and the market admits "no free lunch", then there exists an equivalent martingale measure.

(iii) If the price process is defined on a countably generated probability space, taking values in L^p space, then the "no free lunch" condition is satisfied if and only if there is an equivalent martingale measure satisfying a q moment condition, where $\frac{1}{p} + \frac{1}{q} = 1$.

Although the work of Kreps and colleagues made significant contributions to the theory of arbitrage pricing, there were still assumptions which limited the applicability. Ideally a more economically natural condition could replace the moment condition on the martingale measure. Delbaen and Schachermayer (2006) discuss many open questions. One particular advance links the existence of an equivalent martingale measure in processes in continuous time or infinite discrete time to a condition of "no free lunch with bounded risk". Unfortunately this result does not hold for price processes which are semi-martingales. Furthermore, there are strong mathematical and economic reasons to assume that the price process is a semi-martingale. In that setting the no free lunch with bounded risk is replaced by a no free lunch with vanishing risk, where risk disappears in the limit. The latter is stronger than the former, but is weaker than a no arbitrage condition. So Schachermayer (2010 a,b), and Delbaen and Schachermayer (2006) have a general statement of the fundamental theorem:

Assume the price process is a locally bounded real-valued semi-martingale. There is a martingale measure which is equivalent to the original measure if and only if the price process satisfies the no free lunch with vanishing risk condition.

Yan (1998) brought the results even closer to the desired form. The concept of allowable trading strategies was introduced, where the trader remains liquid during the trading interval. The Yan formulation yields the result:

> Let the price process be a positive semi-martingale. There is a martingale measure which is equivalent to the original measure if and only if the price process satisfies the no free lunch with vanishing risk condition with respect to allowable trading strategies.

Another term for an equivalent martingale measure is a risk-neutral measure. Prices of assets depend on their risk, with a premium required for riskier assets. The advantage of the equivalent martingale or risk-neutral measure is that risk premia are incorporated into the expectation with respect to that measure. Under the risk-neutral measure all assets have the same expected value — the risk-free rate. The stock price process discounted by the risk-free rate is a martingale under the risk-neutral measure. This simplification is important in the valuation of assets such as options and is a component of the famous Black–Scholes (1973) formula. Of course, the risk-neutral measure is an artificial concept, with important implications for the theory of pricing. The actual risk-neutral measure used for price adjustment must be determined from economic reasoning.

The separating hyperplane arguments underlying the results linking arbitrage and no free lunch to martingale measures have an analogy in theorems of the alternative for discrete time and discrete space arbitrage pricing models. In theorems of the alternative competing systems of equalities/inequalities are posed, with only one system having a solution. A famous such theorem is due to A. Tucker (1956). Kallio and Ziemba (2007) used Tucker's Theorem of the Alternative to derive known and some new arbitrage pricing results. The competing systems define arbitrage on the one hand and the existence of risk-neutral probabilities on the other hand. For a frictionless market the Fundamental Theorem of Asset pricing is established using matrix arguments for the discrete time and discrete space price process:

If at each stage an asset exists with strictly positive return (there exists a trading strategy), then arbitrage does not exist if and only if there exists an equivalent martingale measure.

Although the discrete time and space setting is limiting, it is used in practice as an approximation to the continuous process. Obviously there are considerable computational advantages with a discrete process, and assumptions required for its implementation are few. In the general setting the fundamental theorem posits the existence of a risk-neutral measure. Actually finding such a measure requires additional assumptions. In the discrete setting, the equations for calculating the probabilities in the measure can be solved. This is analogous to the option pricing models, where in the Black–Scholes approach strong distribution assumptions are required to get the pricing formula, but the binomial lattice approach obtains option prices with a linear programming algorithm. Even from a theory perspective, the discrete time and space extension to more complex financial markets is feasible since the mathematics is based on systems of equations. In Kallio and Ziemba the equivalence between no arbitrage and the existence of a martingale measure is extended to markets with various imperfections.

The no arbitrage condition is fundamental to much of the theory of efficient capital markets. However, it is important to acknowledge the existence of arbitrage opportunities in actual markets. Examples are the Nikkei put warrant arbitrage discussed in Shaw *et al.* (1995), and the racetrack arbitrages discussed by Hausch and Ziemba (1990a, 1990b). Investors exhibit behavioral biases which can lead to mispricing and arbitrage. Usually over/under pricing is temporary, but correctly identifying those events and using them for financial advantage has attracted attention.

Readings

Black, F. and Scholes, M. (1973). The pricing of options and corporate liabilities, *Journal of Political Economy* **81**(3): 637–654.

Delbaen, F. and Schachermayer, W. (2006). *The Mathematics of Arbitrage.* Springer Finance. Berlin: Springer-Verlag.

Dempster, A. P., Laird, N. M. and Rubin, D. B. (1977). Maximum Likelihood from Incomplete Data via the EM Algorithm, *Journal of the Royal Statistical Society (Series B)*, **39**: 1–38.

Fama, E. F. (1968). Risk, Return and equilibrium: Some clarifying comments, *Journal of Finance* **23**(1): 29–40.

Fama, E. F. and French, F. (1992). The cross-section of expected stock returns, *Journal of Finance* **23**(1): 427–466.

Harrison, J. M. and Kreps, D. M. (1979). Martingales and arbitrage in multiperiod securities markets, *Journal of Economic Theory* **20**(3): 381–408.

Harrison, J. M. and Pliska, S. R. (1981). Martingales and stochastic integrals in the theory of continuous trading, *Stochastic Processes and their Applications* **11**(3): 215–260.

Hausch, D. B. and Ziemba, W. T. (1990a). Arbitrage strategies for cross track betting on major horseraces, *Journal of Business* **LXIII**: 61–78.

Hausch, D. B. and Ziemba, W. T. (1990b). Locks at the racetrack, *Interfaces* **20**(3): 41–48.

Jacobs, B. L. and Levy, K. N. (1988). Disentangling equity return regularities: New insights and investment opportunities, *Financial Analysts Journal* **May/June**, 44, 18–43.

Kahn, M. A. and Sun, Y. (1997). The capital asset pricing model and arbitrage pricing model: A unification. *Proceedings of the National Academy of Sciences of the United States of America*, 94: 4229–4232.

Kallio, M. and Ziemba, W. T. (2007). Using Tucker's theorem of the alternative to provide a framework for proving basic arbitrage results, *Journal of Banking and Finance* **31**: 2281–2302.

Lintner, J. (1965). The valuation of risk assets and the selection of risky investments in stock portfolios and capital budgets, *Review of Economics and Statistics* **47**(1): 13–37.

Markowitz, H. M. (1952). Portfolio Selection, *Journal of Finance* **7**(1): 77–91.

Markowitz, H. M. (1959). *Portfolio Selection: Efficient Diversification of Investments.* New York: John Wiley & Sons.

Modigliani, F. and Miller, M. (1958). The cost of capital, corporation finance and the theory of investment, *American Economic Review* **48**(3): 261–297.

Mossin, J. (1966). Equilibrium in a capital asset market, *Econometrica* **34**(4): 768–783.

Rosenberg, B. (1974). Extra- market components of covariance in securities markets, *Journal of Financial and Quantitative Analysis* **9**(2): 263–274.

Rosenberg, B., Reid, K. and Lanstein, R. (1985). Persuasive evidence of market inefficiency, *Journal of Portfolio Management* **11**(3): 9–16.

Ross, S. A. (1976). The arbitrage theory of capital asset pricing, *Journal of Economic Theory* **13**(3): 341–360.

Schachermayer, W. (2010a). The fundamental theorem of asset pricing, in *Encyclopedia of Quantitative Finance*, R. Cont (ed.), **2**: 792–801, New York: Wiley.

Schachermayer, W. (2010b). Risk neutral pricing, *Encyclopedia of Quantitative Finance* in R. Cont (ed.), **4**: 1581–1585. New York: Wiley.

Schwartz, S. L. and Ziemba, W. T. (2000). Predicting returns on the Tokyo stock exchange, in *Security Market Imperfections in Worldwide Equity Markets*, D. B. Keim and W. T. Ziemba (eds.), Cambridge: Cambridge University Press, 492–511.

Sharpe, W. F. (1964). Capital asset prices: A theory of market equilibrium under conditions of risk, *Journal of Finance* **19**(3): 425–442.

Shaw, J., Thorp, E. O. and Ziemba, W. T. (1995). Convergence to efficiency of the Nikkei put warrant market of 1989–90, *Applied Mathematical Finance* **2**: 243–271.

Treynor, J. L. (1961). Market Value, Time, and Risk. Unpublished manuscript.

Treynor, J. L. (1962). Toward a Theory of Market Value of Risky Assets. Unpublished manuscript. A final version was published in 1999, in *Asset Pricing and Portfolio Performance: Models, Strategy and Performance Metrics*, R. A. Korajczyk (ed.), London: Risk Books, 15–22.

Tucker, A. (1956). Dual systems of homogeneous linear relations, in *Linear Inequalities and Related Systems, Annals of Mathematics Studies*, H. Kuhn, and A. Tucker (eds.), **38**, Princeton: Princeton University Press.

Yan, J. A. (1998). A new look at the fundamental theorem of asset pricing, *Journal of Korean Mathematical Society* **35**: 659–673.

Ziemba, W. T. and Schwartz, S. L. (1991). *Invest Japan: The Structure, Performance and Opportunities of Japan's Stock, Bond and Fund Markets.* Chicago: Probus Publishing.

Appendix A: Fundamentals of Asset Pricing

Capital Asset Pricing Model (CAPM)

The CAPM states that the market portfolio is mean-variance efficient.

For any asset,

$$E[r_j] = r_f + \alpha_j(E[r_M] - r_f),$$

where r_j is the rate of return on asset j, r_f is the risk-free rate and r_M is the market rate of return.

We make the following assumptions:

A1: All investors have mean-variance preferences.

A2: There is a risk-free asset with return r_f.

A3: Investors have homogeneous expectations. This means that everybody has the same beliefs about the return distribution of every asset.

These assumptions immediately imply the following results:

1. The efficient frontier (namely, the straight line through r_f and T — the tangency portfolio) is the same for every investor.
2. Furthermore, for every asset, the weight in T must be the same as in the whole

$$\text{market: } w_j^T = \frac{Market\ Cap_j}{\sum_j Market\ Cap_j}.$$

3. In equilibrium, all risky assets must belong to T.
4. Two fund separation: every investor allocates his wealth between two portfolios: the risk-free asset and the Tangency portfolio.
5. Hence, the Market portfolio is the Tangency portfolio. The CAPM states that the Market portfolio is mean-variance efficient.

Capital market line (CML)

All individual optimal portfolios plot along the CML. For an efficient portfolio p, (i.e., $p \in$ CML),

$$E[r_p] = r_f + \frac{E[r_M] - r_f}{\sigma_M} \times \sigma_p,$$

p is a combination of the risk-free and the market portfolio, thus $\sigma_p = w_M \sigma_M$.

Security market line

We have that for any asset j (not necessarily on the CML)

$$E[r_j] - r_f = \frac{Cov(r_j, r_M)}{Var[r_M]}(E[r_M] - r_f),$$

or

$$SML: E[r_j] = r_f + \beta_j(E[r_M] - r_f).$$

This applies to every single asset or portfolio.

Arbitrage pricing theory (APT) and factor models

Assume that the return on stock j is generated by K random variables called risk factors: $r_j = \alpha_j + \sum_{k=1}^{K} \beta_{kj} F_k + \varepsilon_j$.

Assumptions:

$$A1: E[\varepsilon_j] = 0, \quad \forall j,$$
$$A2: Cov(F_k, \varepsilon_j) = 0, \quad \forall k, j,$$
$$A3: Cov(\varepsilon_i, \varepsilon_j) = 0, \quad \forall j \neq i.$$

Consider an exact K-factor structure:

$$r_j = \alpha_j + \sum_{k=1}^{K} \beta_{kj} F_k.$$

Then, if there are no arbitrage opportunities,

$$E[r_j] = r_f + \sum_{k=1}^{K} \beta_{kj}(E[F_k] - r_f).$$

Consider the general K-factor structure with noise

$$r_j = \alpha_j + \sum_{k=1}^{K} \beta_{kj} F_k + \varepsilon_j.$$

If there is no arbitrage opportunity, then a linear pricing relation will hold approximately for most of the assets in a large economy

$$E[r_j] \approx r_f + \sum_{k=1}^{K} \beta_{kj}(E[F_k] - r_f).$$

The approximation is in the sense that

$$\lim_{n \to \infty} \frac{1}{n} \sum_{j=1}^{n} \left((E[r_j] - r_f) - \sum_{k=1}^{K} \beta_{kj}(E[F_k] - r_f) \right)^2 = 0.$$

Fama and French model

Fama and French (1993) propose the following three-factor asset pricing model:

$$E[r_j] - r_f = \beta_{jM}(E[r_M] - r_f) + \beta_{js}E[SMB] + \beta_{jh}E[HML].$$

Factor mimicking portfolio

Consider a factor mimicking portfolio h that solves

$$\min_{h} \frac{1}{2} h' \Sigma h$$

$$\text{st: } h' \beta = 1.$$

This is the portfolio that minimizes asset return residual variance subject to having unit exposure to the factor β. When the portfolio h is normalized such that $h'e = 1$.

Pricing in complete markets

Two general pricing frameworks in complete markets: for S states of nature, $x(s)$ the payoff, and $p^{ad}(s)$ the Arrow–Debreu price in state $s \in S$

- Arrow–Debreu pricing:

$$p = \sum_{s=1}^{S} x(s) \times p^{ad}(s).$$

- Risk-neutral pricing:

$$p = \frac{E^Q[x]}{1 + r_f}.$$

The market is complete if there exists one Arrow–Debreu price for each possible state of nature, that is, if we can compute $p^{ad}, \forall s$. The reason why market completeness is important is that in arbitrage-free complete markets every financial contract has a unique arbitrage-free price. If the market is complete, any complex security (i.e., any cash flow stream) can be replicated and priced as a portfolio of AD securities.

The Arrow–Debreu pricing formula for any complex security is

$$p = \sum_{s=1}^{S} x(s) \times p^{ad}(s),$$

where $x(s)$ is the payoff in state s.

Define

$$\pi^Q(s) = \frac{p^{ad}(s)}{\sum\limits_{s=1}^{S} p^{ad}(s)},$$

where $\pi^Q(s)$ form a legitimate set of probabilities.

The risk-neutral pricing formula is

$$p = \frac{E^Q[x]}{1 + r_f}.$$

The function Q that defines the probabilities $\pi^Q(s)$ is known as Risk-Neutral probability measure, or Subjective probability measure, or Equivalent Martingale measure. Formally, a probability measure Q is a Risk-neutral probability measure if:

(i) $\pi^Q(s) > 0, \forall s$.

(ii) Equation $p = \frac{E^Q[x]}{1+r_f}$ holds for all securities.

The fundamental theorems of asset pricing

(*First fundamental theorem of asset pricing*)

There exists a risk-neutral probability measure Q if and only if there are no arbitrage opportunities.

(*Second fundamental theorem of asset pricing*)

Assume that the market is arbitrage free. Then, the market is complete if and only if the risk-neutral measure is unique.

Fundamental asset pricing equation

Consider a two-period consumption model. The investor chooses the quantity (x) of the security to buy today (t) to maximize the utility of consumption (c). The problem is

$$\max_{z} U(c_t) + E_t[\delta U(c_{t+1})]$$

$$s.\, t.\; c_t + xp_t = e_t$$
$$c_{t+1} = e_{t+1} + xy_{t+1}$$

where p_t is the price of the security, y_{t+1} is the total payoff, and e is an exogenous endowment the investor receives each period.

The first order condition, the central equation in asset pricing, is written as

$$p_t = E_t[m_{t+1}y_{t+1}],$$

with

$$m_{t+1} \equiv \delta \frac{U'(c_{t+1})}{U'(c_t)}.$$

The random variable m is called stochastic discount factor (SDF), pricing kernel, or marginal rate of substitution. The important point is that one single m prices all assets.

Asset price distributions

Consider the security price P_t, $t = 1, \ldots$ and the rate of return $Y_t = \ln(P_t)$, $t = 1, \ldots$. A standard assumption following from a Brownian motion assumption on price dynamics is normality of returns: $Y_t \sim N(\mu_t, \sigma_t^2)$. So

$$f(y_t) = \frac{1}{\sqrt{2\pi\sigma_t^2}} e^{\frac{(y_t - \mu_t)^2}{2\sigma_t^2}}$$

There is empirical evidence and theoretical models which contradict normality. If the financial market is defined by a finite number of states: $\{S_j, j = 1, \ldots, M\}$, then the normality assumption within a state is closer to reality. So the returns distribution conditional on the state is $Y_{S_j} \sim N(\mu_{S_j}, \sigma_{S_j}^2)$. In that case the marginal distribution of returns (not knowing the state) is a mixture of normals:

$$f(y_t) = \gamma_1 f_1(y_t) \cdots + \gamma_M f_M(y_t).$$

The mixing parameters are typically state distribution probabilities defined from a Markov state switching model. The Expectation-Maximization (EM) algorithm is used to estimate the conditional returns distribution and Markov transition parameters.

EM algorithm

Consider a random variable X, whose distribution at time t is defined by $X_t = \mu_{S_t} + \sigma_{S_t}\varepsilon$, where $\varepsilon \sim N(0,1)$ and S_t is the state or regime at time t. It is usually considered that the actual regimes are hidden and the observable variables are a reflection of the unobservable regimes. The unobservable regimes can be defined as parameters which need to be estimated in addition to the coefficients within regime. The standard estimation method is an adaptation of the EM algorithm (Dempster, 1977), which consists of two steps, the E-Step (estimation of the unknown states/regimes) and the M-Step (maximization of the likelihood conditional on the estimated regimes). Given an initial condition, the two steps alternate in updating parameters. To describe the algorithm used to estimate a regime-switching model, we provide a generic version of the EM algorithm. Assume there is a finite number of regimes $\{S_t = j, j = 1, \ldots, m\}$ and the regimes follow a Markov chain with transition probability matrix $P = (p_{ij})$. Let Θ be the set of parameters $\{\mu_{S_t}, \sigma_{S_t}, P\}$ for the model, X the sequence of observations of the variable $\{X_t\}$ over time, and Y the sequence of unobservable regimes $\{S_t\}$ over time. Denote $\mathcal{Y}$ the space of all possible regime sequences for the time period. The marginal maximum log-likelihood is expressed as: $\max_\Theta \{\ln(\sum_{Y \in \mathcal{Y}} P(X, Y; \Theta))\}$, where $P(X, Y; \Theta)$ is the joint probability distribution function of X and Y.

An iterative algorithm can be designed as follows:

(0) Set the number of regimes at m. This determines the number of parameters in the regime switching model.

(1) E-step: Set an initial value Θ_0 for the true parameter set Θ, calculate the conditional distribution function, $Q(Y) = P(Y|X; \Theta_0)$, and determine the expected log-likelihood, $E^Q[\ln P(X, Y; \Theta)]$.

(2) M-step: Maximize the expected log-likelihood with respect to the conditional distribution of the hidden variable to obtain an improved estimate of Θ. The improved estimate is:

$$\Theta_1 = argmax_\Theta \{E^Q[\ln P(X, Y; \Theta)]\}$$

with Θ_1 as the new initial value for Θ, return to the E-Step.

In the E-step, given the observed data and current estimate of the parameter set, the hidden data are estimated using the conditional expectation. After estimating the parameters, a dynamic programming algorithm is applied to characterize the prevailing regime in each period by maximizing the joint probability of regimes given the observed data.

Section A Exercises

[A1] Assume there is a risky asset, the S&P Index, with the market at a point in time being in one of two regimes: bull and bear. The regimes are driven by a Markov switching process. Within each regime the risky rates of return are assumed to be normally distributed. Collect daily data for the $Y = $ S&P 500 Index for the period 31 July 2004 to 31 July 2014, and let $X = \ln Y$ be the rates of return.

(a) Estimate the parameters in the rate of return distribution without considering regimes.

(b) Use the EM algorithm to estimate the parameters in the regime switching model.

(c) Find the mean squared error for predicted rates of return for the without regimes and regimes models. Comment on the benefits of regimes.

[A2] APT is defined by equations for the return on risky assets.

(a) Give the equations for APT using factors.

(b) Give the equations for APT using factor risk premiums.

[A3] APT relies on the assumption that we can construct so-called pure factor portfolios.

(a) Explain the pure factor portfolio and the necessary conditions for applying the no-arbitrage argument.

(b) Explain how to replicate an asset using pure factor portfolios.

[A4] Securities can be priced either using a market equilibrium argument or a no-arbitrage argument.

(a) Explain the relationship between CAPM and APT and the argument behind each of the models.

(b) What is the minimum number of factors needed in order to explain the expected returns of a group of 8 securities, if the securities have no market specific risk?

[A5] Consider a two factor model for the returns of three stocks.

$$\begin{bmatrix} X_1 \\ X_2 \\ X_2 \end{bmatrix} = \begin{bmatrix} 0.07 & 1.0 & 1.0 \\ 0.06 & 3.0 & 2.0 \\ 0.03 & 2.5 & 0.5 \end{bmatrix} \begin{bmatrix} 1 \\ F_1 \\ F_2 \end{bmatrix} + \begin{bmatrix} \varepsilon_1 \\ \varepsilon_2 \\ \varepsilon_3 \end{bmatrix}.$$

Assume the factors have mean 0 and a variance of 0.01, and ε_i have mean 0, are uncorrelated, and $\sigma^2(\varepsilon_1) = 0.01$, and covariance matrix $\begin{bmatrix} 0.01 & 0 & 0 \\ 0 & 0.04 & 0 \\ 0 & 0 & 0.02 \end{bmatrix}$. Portfolios can constructed from the assets with weights in each factor (w_1, w_2).

(a) Find the expected returns of the assets.

(b) Find the variance–covariance matrix of the return to the three assets.

(c) Construct one portfolio with $w_1 = 0, w_2 = 1$ and another portfolio with $w_1 = 1, w_2 = 0$. Compute the expected return and risk premiums of these two portfolios.

(d) Consider a fourth asset with the following equation:

$$X_4 = 0.07 + F_1 + F_2.$$

Does this give rise to an arbitrage opportunity, if we assume that the APT holds?

[A6] Consider three assets with payoffs and prices

	State 1	State 2	State 3	Price
Asset 1	2	0	0	1.2
Asset 2	3	1	0	1.8
Asset 3	1	0.5	0.5	1.2
Prob	0.25	0.50	0.25	

(a) If a fourth asset has state Payoffs $(1, 9, 3)$, compute the asset price using the risk-neutral pricing method.

(b) If a bank will sell this asset for $p_4 = 2.0$ should you purchase it?

(c) Compute the price of the fourth asset using the pricing kernel.

[A7] The portfolio return that solves $\max_R E(\ln(1 + R))$ is known as the growth optimal portfolio. The pricing kernel equation is $1 = E(m(1 + R))$, where m is the SDF and $(1 + R)$ is the gross return.

(a) Show that the negative of the mean log discount factor must be larger than any mean return, $-E(\ln(m)) > E(\ln(1 + R))$.

(b) How is it possible that $E(\ln(1 + R))$ is bounded? What about returns of the form $R = (1 - \alpha)R_f + \alpha R_M$ for arbitrarily large α, where R_f is the risk free return and R_M is the market return?

[A8] Consider a two-period consumption model where there is a security with price p_t at time t, an exogenous endowment e_t and a terminal return y_{t+1}. The investor chooses x, the amount of the security to purchase, to maximize the expected utility of consumption c. The problem is

$$\max_x E[u(c_t) + \delta u(c_{t+1})]$$

$$\text{s.t. } c_t = e_t - x p_t$$

$$c_{t+1} = e_{t+1} + x y_{t+1}.$$

(a) What are the first order and second order conditions.

(b) What property of the utility will ensure a maximum exists.

(c) Compute the pricing kernel for the power utility $u(c) = \frac{c^{1-\gamma}}{1-\gamma}$.

[A9] If m_t is the pricing kernel and $(1 + R_t)$ is the gross return on a security, the fundamental pricing equation is $E[m_t(1 + R_t)] = 1$.

(a) If a risk-free security costs \$1 and has a gross return $(1 + r_t)$ write the pricing equation for this security.

(b) Use the pricing equation to express the excess return on a risky security $\{E[R_t] - r_t\}$ in terms of the covariance of marginal utility and returns.

[A10] In a two-period model suppose an investor determines the quantities of stock (x_1) and bond (x_2) to purchase to maximize current and next period consumption. Let p_i, $i = 1, 2$ be the deterministic prices, $1 + R_i$, $i = 1, 2$ the random gross returns for the stock/bond, and assume w is the exogenous initial wealth. The problem is

$$\max_{x_1, x_2}\{u(c_1) + E[\delta u(C_2)]\}$$

s.t.

$$c_1 + x_1 p_1 + x_2 p_2 = w$$
$$C_2 = x_1(1 + R_1) + x_2(1 + R_2).$$

(a) Give the first order conditions for maximization.
(b) For utility $u(c) = \ln(c)$ write the pricing kernel.
(c) Assume there are four scenarios with the following bond return and consumption

	Scenario			
	S_1	S_2	S_3	S_4
C_2	90	100	105	115
R_2	0	9	10	11
Prob	0.1	0.3	0.5	0.1

If $\delta = 0.99$ and $c_1 = 100$, compute the price of the bond.

[A11] Consider the information on two stocks and the market portfolio

Asset	Standard deviation of returns	Correlation of returns with market portfolio return
A	0.5	0.7
B	0.6	−0.3
Market Portfolio	0.2	1.0

The rate of return on the market is 6% and the risk-free rate is 2%.

(a) Calculate the SML for CAPM.

(b) Calculate the beta coefficients for the two securities.

(c) If the rates of return on the securities are 5.5% and 4% respectively, what can you conclude about the securities?

[A12] The law of one price states that: *A security must have a single price, no matter how that security is created. For example, if an option can be created using two different sets of underlying securities, then the total price for each would be the same.*

(a) Show that the law of one price implies that price is a linear function of payoff implies.

(b) Show that the absence of arbitrage implies the law of one price?

(c) If the law of one price holds in the population, must it hold in a sample drawn from that population?

[A13] Consider the CAPM, where a mean-variance efficient point with return r satisfies

$$r_n = r^* + w r_o$$

where r^* is the minimum variance portfolio return and r_o is a zero beta return

(a) For a discount factor $m = a + b r_m$, do we have to rule out the case of risk neutrality?

(b) Suppose the CAPM is true, $m = a - b R_m$ prices a set of assets, and there is a risk-free rate r_f. Find r^* in terms of the moments of r_m, r_f.

(c) If you express the mean-variance frontier as a linear combination of factor-mimicking portfolios from a factor model, do the relative weights of the various factor portfolios in the mean-variance efficient return change as you sweep out the frontier, or do they stay the same?

(d) For an arbitrary mean-variance efficient return of the form $r^* + wr_o$, find its zero-beta return and zero-beta rate. Show that your rate reduces to the risk-free rate when there is one.

(e) When the economy is risk neutral, and if there is no risk-free rate, show that the zero-beta, minimum-variance, and constant-mimicking portfolio returns are again all equivalent, though not equal to the risk-free rate. (In this case, the mean-variance frontier is just the minimum-variance point.)

[A14] Properties of univariate log-normal distributions. The notion that random investment returns are subject to limited liability in the sense that the investor can lose no more than his initial outlay leads to the study of distributions whose outcomes are never negative. The log-normal distribution is such a distribution and it arises naturally from modified central limit theorems.

If X is an essentially positive variate and $Y = \log X$ has a normal distribution with mean μ and variance σ^2, then X has a log-normal distribution with density

$$f(x) = \frac{1}{x\sigma\sqrt{2\pi}} e^{-\frac{(\log x - \mu)^2}{2\sigma^2}}, \, x > 0.$$

The log-normal variables arise in cases where the variable is a product of i.i.d. elementary variables.

(a) Use the moment generating function $\psi(t) = E[e^{tX}]$ to show that

$$E(X) = e^{\mu + \frac{\sigma^2}{2}}, \quad var(X) = e^{2\mu + \sigma^2}[e^{\sigma^2} - 1].$$

The log-normal distribution is not closed under addition. However the log-normal distribution has a number of useful multiplicative properties since logs of multiplicative functions are additive.

(b) Suppose $X_i \sim LN(\mu_i, \sigma_i^2)$ are independent, $i = 1, \ldots,$ $n < \infty$. Show that $\prod_{i=1}^n X_i \sim LN(\sum \mu_i, \sum \sigma_i^2)$.

(c) Suppose $X_i \sim LN(\mu_i, \sigma_i^2)$ are independent, $i = 1, \ldots,$ $n < \infty; a, b_1, \ldots, b_n$, and $c > 0$ are constants ($c = e^a$). Show that $c \prod_i X_i^{b_i} \sim LN(a + \sum b_i \mu_i, \sum b_i^2 \sigma_i^2)$.

(d) Show that if $X \sim LN(\mu, \sigma^2)$, $\frac{1}{X} \sim LN(-\mu, \sigma^2)$.

(e) Suppose $X_i \sim LN(\mu_i, \sigma_i^2)$ are independent, $i = 1, 2$. Show that

$$\frac{X_1}{X_2} \sim LN(\pi_1 - \mu_2, \sigma_1^2 + \sigma_2^2).$$

[A15] Properties of multivariate log-normal distributions. Suppose $Y_1, \ldots, Y_M$ have the multivariate normal distribution $N(\mu, \Sigma)$, where μ is the mean vector and Σ is the covariance matrix. Then the vector $X' = (X_1, \ldots, X_m) = (e^{Y_1}, \ldots, e^{Y_m})$ has a multi-variate log-normal distribution $X \sim\sim LN(\mu, \Sigma)$.

(a) Show the density is $f(X) = \dfrac{1}{(2\pi)^{\frac{m}{2}} |\Sigma|^{\frac{1}{2}} \prod X_i} \exp\{-\frac{1}{2}\}$ $(\log X - \mu)' \Sigma^{-1}(\log X - \mu)$, where $\log X = (\log X_1, \ldots, \log X_m)$.

(b) Use the moment generating function to show the mean of X is $(e^{\mu_1 + \frac{\sigma_1^2}{2}}, \ldots, e^{\mu_m + \frac{\sigma_m^2}{2}})'$.

(c) Show that the covariance of (X_i, X_j) is $\{\mu_i + \mu_j + \frac{1}{2}(\sigma_{ii} + \sigma_{jj} + 2\sigma_{ij}) - exp\{\mu_i + \mu_j + \frac{1}{2}(\sigma_{ii} + \sigma_{jj})\}\}$.

(d) Suppose $a, b_1, \ldots, b_n$, and $c > 0$ are constants ($c = e^a$). Show that $c \prod_i X_i^{b_i} \sim LN(a + b'\mu, b'\Sigma b)$.

Exercise Source Notes

Exercises [A15] and [A16] were adapted from Ziemba–Vickson (1975) pp. 353 # 20 and 354 # 21. The other exercises were provided by Leonard MacLean.

SECTION B: UTILITY THEORY

Decision makers in financial markets are faced with a variety of opportunities and must decide how much capital to allocate to the various assets in the opportunity set at points in time. Investing in assets produces returns (gains/losses), resulting from the price changes. The returns on a unit of capital invested in assets are uncertain, that is, the return vector is a random variable. The basic information input to the decision on how much to invest in each asset is the distribution for the return vector. In Section A, some models for the dynamics of the stochastic return vector were considered. Assuming that the return distributions are known, the investment decisions are based on preferences for changes in wealth or accumulated wealth. To structure the decision process, a theory of preferences is required. The theory of preferences concerns the ability to represent a preference structure with a real-valued function. This has been achieved by mapping it to the mathematical index called *utility*. To put the preference relation for an individual into a theory of utility the following axioms were proposed by Von Neumann and Morgenstern (1944) and Savage (1954).

Let S be the set (possibly infinite) of alternatives for a system each having a monetary payoff with a known probability. There are four axioms of the expected utility theory that define a *rational* decision maker. They are completeness, transitivity, independence and continuity.

Completeness: For any two alternatives A and B in S, either A is preferred to B or B is preferred to A or there is indifference between the alternatives.

Transitivity: For alternatives A, B and C, if A is preferred to B and B is preferred to C, then A is preferred to C.

Continuity: For alternatives A, B and C, if A is preferred to B is preferred to C, then there exists a probability π such that B is as good as (indifferent to) $\pi A + (1 - \pi)C$.

Independence: For alternatives A, B and C, with A preferred to B, for $\alpha \in (0, 1]$, $\alpha A + (1 - \alpha)C$ is preferred to $\alpha B + (1 - \alpha)C$.

If the four preference axioms are satisfied then the preference relationship can be expressed in terms of a utility function $u(X(A))$, where $X(A)$ is the random monetary payoff from an alternative A and $F_{X(A)}$ is the distribution for $X(A)$.

Expected Utility Theorem: For any two alternatives A and B in S, A is preferred to B if and only if $Eu(X(A)) > Eu(X(B))$ and there is indifference iff $Eu(X(A)) = Eu(X(B))$.

A general proof of the expected utility theorem is provided by Fishburn (1969). The fact that preferences can be defined by a utility function is very useful for the analysis of preferences and the decision problem of choosing the best alternative. In following this approach it is important to keep in mind that it is assumed that decision makers satisfy the axioms in stating their preferences. This is referred to as rational decision making (Savage, 1954).

Expected utility theory implies that rational individuals act as though they were maximizing expected utility, and that allows for the fact that many individuals are risk averse, meaning that the individual would refuse a fair gamble (a fair gamble has an expected value of zero). If $X(A)$ is a random outcome and $X(B)$ is a random outcome with distribution equal to that of $X(A) + \varepsilon$, where ε is uncorrelated noise, then $X(A)$ is preferred to $X(B)$ by any risk averter. So there is a class of decision makers who are averse to risk as characterized by greater uncertainty. With the inverse cumulative distributions $F_{X(A)}^{-1}$ and $F_{X(B)}^{-1}$, let $T(\alpha) = \int_0^\alpha [F_{X(A)}^{-1}(p) - F_{X(B)}^{-1}(p)]dp =$ the area between the distributions in the α tail. Then $T(\alpha) \geq 0, 0 \leq \alpha \leq 1, T(1) = 0$, which follows from the greater variability of $X(B)$, which has the same mean as $X(A)$. Going back to the expected utility theorem, this class has a particular type of utility function. A utility function u for which:

$$\int_0^\alpha [F_{X(A)}^{-1}(p) - F_{X(B)}^{-1}(p)]dp \geq 0, 0 \leq \alpha \leq 1, \text{ implies that}$$
$Eu(X(A)) \geq Eu(X(B))$ for u a concave function
(Rothschild and Stiglitz 1970).

The area/integration condition implies that the utility has decreasing first derivatives (negative second derivatives). So the risk averter has a concave utility. In fact the degree of aversion at an outcome level is defined by the size of the second derivative relative to the first derivative (Pratt 1964; Arrow 1965).

The risk aversion implied by expected utility theory has a shortcoming in that it does not provide a realistic description of risk attitudes to modest stakes. To have realistic risk aversion for large stakes produces virtual risk neutrality for moderate ones. Rabin (2000) presents a theorem that calibrates a relationship between risk attitudes over small and large stakes. The theorem shows that, within the expected utility model, anything but virtual risk neutrality over modest stakes implies manifestly unrealistic risk aversion over large stakes. For example, A person who would for any initial wealth turn down 50–50 lose \$1,000/gain \$1,050 bets would always turn down 50–50 bets of losing \$20,000 or gaining any sum. With utility function u and initial wealth of \$20,000, the first bet implies on a wager of

$1,000$ that $0.5u(19,000) + 0.5u(21,050) < u(20,000)$ and therefore on a wager of $20,000, it follows that $0.5u(0) + 0.5u(220,000) < u(20,000)$. In this sense, expected utility theory can be misleading when analyzing situations involving modest stakes.

A decision that maximizes expected utility also maximizes the probability of the decision's consequences being preferable to some uncertain threshold (Castagnoli and LiCalzi, 1996; Bordley and LiCalzi, 2000; and Bordley and Kirkwood, 2004). In the absence of uncertainty about the threshold, expected utility maximization simplifies to maximizing the probability of achieving some fixed target. If the uncertainty is uniformly distributed, then expected utility maximization becomes expected value maximization. Intermediate cases lead to increasing risk-aversion above some fixed threshold and increasing risk-seeking below a fixed threshold.

There are examples of choice problems where preferences do not satisfy the axioms. The Allais paradox (Allais, 1953), the Ellsberg paradox (Ellsberg, 1961), and the Bergen paradox (Allais and Hagen, 1979) provide well-known contradictions to the expected utility theorem (see also Tversky and Kahneman, 1974). The Allais paradox has received particular attention. From the independence axiom, for alternatives A, B and C, with A preferred to B, then for $\alpha \in (0, 1]$ it follows that $\alpha A + (1 - \alpha)C$ is preferred to $\alpha B + (1 - \alpha)C$. However, it has been experimentally demonstrated that the preference for $\alpha A + (1 - \alpha)C$ over $\alpha B + (1 - \alpha)C$ can be reversed depending on the value of α. The independence axiom is the key to the linearity in probabilities of the expected utility and that property is violated in the Allais paradox.

In expected utility theory, the utilities of outcomes are weighted by their probabilities. It has been shown that people overweight outcomes that are considered certain relative to outcomes which are merely probable, a phenomenon which is labeled the *certainty effect*.

There have been a variety of proposals for dealing with the violation of the independence axiom and the linearity in probabilities. One approach is Prospect Theory (PT) proposed by Kahneman and Tversky (1979, 1984). The bilinear form of expected utility is retained, but probabilities and outcomes are transformed. The value of a prospect, denoted V, is expressed in terms of two scales, π and v. The first scale, π, associates with each probability p, a subjective decision weight $\pi(p)$, which reflects the impact of p on the overall value of the prospect. The second scale, v, assigns to each outcome x a number $v(x)$, which reflects the subjective value of that outcome. The outcomes are defined relative to a reference point, which serves as the zero point of the value scale. Hence, v measures the value of deviations or changes from that reference point. The value function is S-shaped, being convex for losses ($x < 0$) and concave for gains ($x > 0$). This idea dates to Markowitz (1952b) who commented on the Friedman–Savage (1948) utility functions leading to the S-shape.

The basic equation of the theory describes the manner in which π and v are combined to determine the overall value of regular prospects. In a simple binary case, if $(x, p; y, q)$ is a prospect then the value of the prospect is $V(x, p; y, q) = \pi(p)v(x) + \pi(q)v(y)$, where $v(0) = 0, \pi(0) = 0$, and $\pi(1) = 1$. This equation generalizes expected utility theory by relaxing the expectation principle. An axiomatic analysis of this representation is provided in Kahneman and Tversky (1979).

The class of all PT value functions are S-shaped with an inflection point at $x = 0$. Thus, $v' > 0$, $v(x)'' > 0$ for $x < 0$, and $v(x)'' < 0$ for $x > 0$. This is contrasted with the class of all Markowitz (1952) value functions which are reverse S-shaped with an inflection point at $x = 0$. Thus, $v' > 0$, $v''(x) > 0$ for $x > 0$, and $v''(x) < 0$ for $x < 0$. Markowitz's function, like the PT value function, depends on change of wealth. The functions are depicted in Fig. 1.

Levy and Levy (2002) define Prospect Stochastic Dominance (PSD) and the Markowitz Stochastic Dominance (MSD). If Prospect F dominates Prospect G by PSD, then F is preferred over G by any PT S-shaped value function. MSD corresponds to all reverse S-shaped value functions. PSD and MSD are opposite if the two distributions have the same mean: Let F and G have the same mean. Then F dominates G by PSD if and only if G dominates F by MSD.

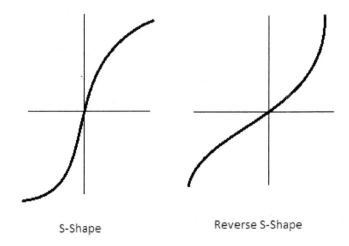

S-Shape   Reverse S-Shape

Fig. 1:   Non-concave utilities.

PT has its critics. Levy and Levy (2002, 2004) cast doubt on the S-shaped value function, based on experimental results. They conducted a set of decision making experiments to determine if the decision behavior of subjects conforms to PT. The focus of their analysis is the S-shape of the value function in PT and contrasted that function with the Markowitz reverse S-shape. With the stochastic dominance approach they take the weighting function as $\pi(p) = p$, so the probabilities are not transformed. In each of the Levy and Levy experiments the subjects' decision behavior supported the reverse S-shape value function and they considered that as evidence against PT, or at least the S-shape value function. By defining stochastic dominance (PSD, MSD) based on the value function while retaining the original probability distribution, the weighting function of PT is not a factor. In Kahneman and Tversky the bi-criteria (value, probability) are both transformed. That is, the decision maker distorts both dimensions. To illustrate this affect, Wakker (2003) analyzes the Levy and Levy experiments using decision weights to transform probabilities based on assumptions of Tversky and Kahneman. The result is that the observed decision behavior in the experiments is consistent with the S-shape of PT.

In the experiments conducted by Levy and Levy neither of the competing gambles were preferred by second order stochastic dominance (SSD). Baltussen *et al.* (2006) augmented the LL tasks with a third gamble which by SSD is preferred to either original gamble, with all gambles having the same expectation. The empirical evidence supports SSD as opposed to either PSD or MSD.

The support for the S-shaped function as obtained by Kahneman and Tversky (1979) is actually due to the certainty effect. Obviously, different individuals have different preferences. Classes of functions: concave, S-shaped, reverse S-shaped, represent contrasting perspectives on risk. There is evidence to support different utilities for gains and losses, which are defined with respect to a reference point. When considering gains and losses separately the utility is concave for gains and convex for losses (Abdellaoui, 2000; Abdellaoui *et al.*, 2007) as implied by PT. However, evidence indicates individuals are less sensitive to probability differences when choosing among mixed gambles than when choosing among either gain or loss gambles (Wu and Markle, 2008).

An interesting perspective on risk assessment comes from the "risk matrix" used in reliability engineering, where value and probability are on a log scale (Fig. 2).

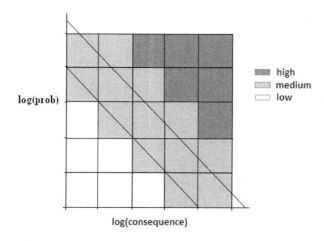

Fig. 2: Risk matrix.

A description of the Risk Matrix is provided in Krishnamurthy (2014). The classification of risk is based on the combination of outcome and probability. There are criteria for a consistent classification defined in Cox (2008). If a benchmark return is identified and a shortfall event is falling below the benchmark, then the probability of a shortfall and the shortfall size are the bi-criteria defining risk:

(*Prob and size of shortfall*). Assume there is a utility or preference for shortfalls, that is, for shortfall of size x the preference is $u(x)$. For example, in the PT case where the benchmark is set to 0 and shortfalls are $x < 0$, then $u(x) = -u(-x)$ is a possibility. If $g(x|short)$ is the conditional distribution of shortfalls and Λ is the shortfall probability, then the expected shortfall utility or risk score is $RPN = E(u(X))\Lambda$, where $E(u(X)) = \int u(x)g(x|short)$ and $\Lambda = \Pr[short]$. The logarithm transformation gives $\ln(RPN) = \ln[E(u(X))] + \ln[\Lambda]$. The score $RPN = [Avg\,Size] \times [Prob]$ is consistent with first order stochastic dominance. The equation $\ln(Avg\,Size) + \ln(Prob) = constant$ is used to define normal and abnormal pairs, as shown in Fig. 2.

The stochastic dominance definitions provide a way to characterize consistent preferences for risk. A standard technique for defining risk preferences is mean-variance analysis (Markowitz, 1952a). Assuming a normal distribution for outcome returns, the mean-variance rule is consistent with expected utility and SSD (concave utility). So MV and PT are not compatible when considering the preferences between two alternatives. However, Levy and Levy (2004) establish that the efficient sets (undominated) from second order dominance (MV) and PSD are almost identical when dealing with a mixture of sets of alternatives (diversified portfolios).

The value and utility functions to this point have been a temporal, being concerned with preferences between alternatives. In financial decision making the system is dynamic and the alternatives consist of outcomes such as consumption at points in time. For example, in discrete time the outcome could be the consumption stream $C = (c_1, \ldots, c_t, \ldots, c_T)$. The standard approach to valuing

C is to have $V(C) = \sum_{t=1}^{T} \rho^{t-1} u(c_t)$, for the discount factor ρ. With this form of intertemporal additive and homogeneous utility, the expected utility theory translates readily. However, the problems giving rise to non-expected utility apply to this intertemporal format. An additional problem is that the two distinct aspects of preference, intertemporal substitutability and relative risk aversion, are intertwined; indeed the elasticity of substitution and the risk aversion parameter are reciprocals of one another.

Epstein and Zin (1989) consider the intertemporal utility issues. They define a general class of preferences which is sufficiently flexible to permit those two aspects of preference to be separated. The utility V is recursive, so that V satisfies the following equation:

$$V(c_1, \ldots, c_T) = W(c_1, \mu(c_2, \ldots, c_T)),$$

where W is an increasing aggregator function and μ is a certainty equivalent. They require that the aggregator function have a constant elasticity of substitution. The certainty equivalent can be any member of a broad class of mean value functionals. A form of continuity is required of the functional.

Epstein and Zin (1989) establish the existence of the intertemporal utility V following from the aggregator W and functional μ.

Readings

Abdellaoui, M. (2000). Parameter-free elicitation of utility and probability weighting functions, *Management Science* **46**(11): 1497–1512.

Abdellaoui, M., Bleichrodt, H. and Paraschiv, C. (2007). Loss aversion under prospect theory: A parameter-free measurement, *Management Science* **53**(10): 1659–1674.

Allais, M. (1953). Le comportement de l'homme rationnel devant le risque: Critique des postulats et axiomes de l'école Américaine, *Econometrica* **21**(4): 503–546.

Allais, M. and Hagen, O. (1979). Expected Utility Hypotheses and the *Allais* Paradox. Dordrecht, Holland: Reidel.

Arrow, K. J. (1965). The theory of risk aversion, in *Aspects of the Theory of Risk Bearing*, Y. J. Saatio, (ed.). Reprinted in *Essays in the Theory of Risk Bearing* (1971). Chicago: Markham Publ. Co., 90–109.

Baltussen, G., Post, T. and van Vliet, P. (2006). Violations of cumulative prospect theory in mixed gambles with moderate probabilities, *Management Science* **52**(8): 1288–1290.

Bordley, R. F. and Kirkwood, C. (2004). Preference analysis with multi-attribute performance targets, *Operations Research* **52**(6): 823–835.

Bordley, R. F. and LiCalzi, M. (2000). Decision analysis using targets instead of utility functions, *Decisions in Economics and Finance* **23**(1): 53–74.

Castagnoli, E. and LiCalzi, M. (1996). Expected utility without utility, *Theory and Decision* **41**, 281–301.

Cox, L. A. (2008). What's wrong with risk matrices? *Risk Analysis* **28**(2): 497–512.

Ellsberg, D. (1961). Risk, ambiguity, and the Savage Axioms, *Quarterly Journal of Economica* **75**(4): 643–669.

Epstein, L. G. and Zin, S. E. (1989). Substitution, risk aversion and the temporal behavior of consumption and asset returns: A theoretical framework, *Econometrica* **57**(4): 937–969.

Fishburn, F. (1969). A general theory of subjective probabilities and expected utilities, *Annals of Mathematical Statistics* **40**(4): 1419–1429.

Friedman, M. and Savage, L. J. (1948). Utility analysis of choices involving risk, *Journal of Political Economy* **56**(4): 279–304.

Kahneman, D. and Tversky, A. (1979). Prospect theory: An analysis of decisions under risk, *Econometricia* **47**(2): 263–291.

Kahneman, D. and Tversky, A. (1984). Choices, values, and frames, *American Psychologist* **39**(4): 314–350.

Krishnamurthy, S. (2014). Quantifying model risk. *Wilmott*, January: 56–59.

Levy, M. and Levy, H. (2002). Prospect theory: Much ado about nothing, *Management Science* **48**(10): 1334–1349.

Levy, M. and Levy, H. (2004). Prospect theory and mean-variance analysis, *Review of Financial Studies* **17**(4): 1015–1041.

Markowitz, H. (1952a). Portfolio selection, *Journal of Finance*, **7**: 77–91.

Markowitz, H. M. (1952b). The utility of wealth, *Journal of Political Economy*, **60**: 151–156.

Pratt, J. W. (1964). Risk aversion in the small and in the large, *Econometrica* **32**(1, 2): 122–136.

Rabin, M. (2000). Risk aversion and expected utility theory: A calibration theorem, *Econometrica* **68**(5): 1281–1292.

Rothschild, M. and Stiglitz, J. (1970). Increasing Risk: 1. A Definition, *Journal of Economic Theory* **3**(2): 225–243.

Savage, L. J. (1954). *The Foundations of Statistics*. New York, Wiley.
Tversky, A. and Kahneman, D. (1974). Judgment under uncertainty: Heuristics and biases. *Science* **185**(4157): 1124–1131.
Von Neumann, J. and Morgenstern, O. (1944). *Theory of Games and Economic Behavior*. Princeton, NJ: Princeton University Press.
Wakker, P. (2003). The data of Levy and Levy (2002) "Prospect Theory: much ado about nothing?" Actually support Prospect Theory, *Management Science* **49**(7): 979–981.
Wu, G. and Markle, A. (2008). An empirical test of gain-loss separability in Prospect Theory, *Management Science* **54**(7): 1322–1335.

Appendix B: Technical Fundamentals for Utility Theory

Utility Function

Consider a set of objects $\mathcal{X}$ and the real line $\mathcal{R}$. If there is a preference relation $\succcurlyeq$ which orders pairs of elements in $\mathcal{X}$, i.e., for $X_1, X_2, \in \mathcal{X}$ either $X_1 \succcurlyeq X_2$ or $X_2 \succcurlyeq X_1$, and the relation is complete, transitive and continuous, then there exists a function $U : \mathcal{X} \to \mathcal{R}$, which gives the corresponding order:

$$X_1 \succcurlyeq X_2 \Leftrightarrow U(X_1) \geq U(X_2).$$

Probability

The elements of $\mathcal{X}$ are often random variables or lotteries. With the probability space (Ω, B, P), then $X \in \mathcal{X}$ is a function $X \colon \Omega \to \mathcal{R}$, which generates a distribution function F_X. So $F_X(x) = P[B_x]$, where $B_x = \{\omega | X(\omega) \leq x\}$.

Stochastic Order

A real random variable X is less than a random variable Y in the "usual stochastic order" if

$$F_X(z) \geq F_Y(z), \quad \text{for all } z \in (-\infty, \infty).$$

Alternatively,

$$F_X^{-1}(\alpha) \leq F_Y^{-1}(\alpha), \quad \text{for all } \alpha \in [0,1].$$

The usual order is first degree or first order stochastic dominance, written as $X \preccurlyeq_1 Y$. It is a partial order, but the class of ordered random variables can be increased by integration of lower orders. So second order stochastic dominance of X and Y is $X \preccurlyeq_2 Y$, where

$$\int_0^\alpha [F_X^{-1}(p) - F_Y^{-1}(p)]dp \leq 0, \quad \text{for all } \alpha \in (0,1].$$

The kth degree ordering of X and Y is $X \preccurlyeq_k Y$, where

$$\int_0^\alpha \cdots \left\{ \int_0^{p_3} \left\{ \int_0^{p_2} [F_X^{-1}(p_1) - F_Y^{-1}(p_1)]dp_1 \right\} dp_2 \right\} \cdots dp_{k-1} \leq 0$$

$$\text{for all } \alpha \in (0,1].$$

A lower order implies all subsequent orders, but the reverse is not true.

Expected Utility

The order based on inverse distribution functions also has an alternative formulation in terms of expected utility. If we have a function u of the random variable X, with distribution F_X, the expected value is

$$E[u(X)] = \int_{-\infty}^\infty u(x)dF(x).$$

Then $X \preccurlyeq_1 Y$ iff $E[u(X)] \leq E[u(Y)]$, for all non-decreasing functions u. So $u^{(1)}(x) = \frac{d}{dx}u(x) \geq 0$.

Also $X \preccurlyeq_2 Y$ iff $E[u(X)] \leq E[u(Y)]$ for all non-decreasing, concave functions u. So $u^{(1)}(x) = \frac{d}{dx}u(x) \geq 0$ and $u^{(2)}(x) = \frac{d}{dx}u^1(x) \leq 0$.

In general, $X \preccurlyeq_n Y$ iff $E[u(X)] \leq E[u(Y)]$ for all u such that $(-1)^c u^{(c)}(x) \leq 0$, for $c = 1, \ldots, n$.

Utility functions with alternating signs on derivatives, $(-1)^c u^{(c)}(x) \leq 0$, for $c = 1, \ldots, n$ characterize types of preference functions. For example $u^{(1)}(x) \geq 0$ and $u^{(2)}(x) \leq 0$ defines concave utilities, where marginal utility is decreasing.

Common Utility Functions

Logarithmic: $u(x) = \log_e(x)$

Power: $u(x) = \dfrac{1}{1-\gamma} x^{1-\gamma}, \gamma < 1.$

Exponential: $u(x) = -e^{-\beta x}.$

Quadratic: $u(x) = ax - bx^2.$

Prospect: $u(x) = (x - k)^\alpha, \; x \geq k > 0, \; 0 < \alpha < 1$
$$= -\lambda(k - x)^\beta, x \leq k, \; \alpha < \beta < 1, \; \lambda > 1.$$

HARA: $u(x) = \dfrac{1}{b-1}[(a + bx)^{\frac{b-1}{b}}], \; b > 0.$

Intertemporal: $u(c_1, c_2) = [c_1^\rho + \beta c_2^\rho]^{\frac{1}{\rho}}, \; 0 \neq \rho < 1, \; 0 < \beta < 1.$

Certainty Equivalent

For wealth w the certainty equivalent of the uncertain return X is the deterministic value $\hat{x}$, where

$$E[u(w + X)] = u(w + \hat{x}).$$

Risk Aversion and concavity

A utility function is concave iff

$$u^{(1)}(x) > 0, \; u^{(2)}(x) < 0.$$

Arrow–Pratt's measure of Absolute Risk Aversion:

$$\rho(x) = -\frac{u^{(2)}(x)}{u^{(1)}(x)}.$$

Arrow–Pratt's measure of Relative Risk Aversion:

$$\rho^*(x) = x\rho(x) = -\frac{xu^{(2)}(x)}{u^{(1)}(x)}.$$

Global Risk Aversion measure:

$$\Upsilon(x_0) = \frac{-x_0 E\{u^{(2)}(x)\}}{E\{u^{(1)}(x)\}},$$

where expectation is with respect to the randomness in x.

Section B Exercises

[B1] If $u(x)$ is a utility for a given order relation, and $v(x) = a + bu(x)$, $a > 0$, then show that $v(x)$ is also a utility for that order relation.

[B2] A consequence of the expected utility theorem is that cardinal utility functions are unique only up to positive linear transformation. Thus $u(w) = a + bv(w)$ for $b >$ represents the same preferences as v. To specify the utility function uniquely one must specify two boundary conditions, such as requiring that u goes through the origin with slope 1, i. e., $u(0) = 0$, $u'(0) = 1$. Determine what a and b must be in this case if $v(w)$ is

(a) $\log(w + w_0)$, where $w_0 > 0$;

(b) $(w + w_0)^\alpha$, where $w_0 > 0$ and $< \alpha < 1$;

(c) $w - \beta w^2, \beta > 0$;

(d) $-e^{-\delta w}, \delta > 0$.

[B3] Prove that

$$\lim_{\gamma \to 1} \frac{x^{1-\gamma} - 1}{1 - \gamma} = \ln(x).$$

[B4] Consider an investor having an initial wealth of \$16 whose utility function for wealth w is $u(w) = w^{\frac{1}{2}}$.

(a) Show that the investor is indifferent between the status quo and the following two gambles:

(i) lose \$7 or gain \$9 with equal probability, and

(ii) lose \$16 with probability 22/80, gain \$48 with probability 1/8 and gain \$9 with probability 3/5.

(b) Will he prefer to accept one or more of these gambles if his initial wealth is \$25?

(c) Change the odds on these gambles so that he is indifferent between each of the gambles and the status quo if his initial wealth is $30.

[**B5**] Consider the gambles in [B4] and let the utility function be

$$u(w) = w^\alpha.$$

For what values of α strictly between 0 and 1 does the investor prefer the status quo, gamble (i), and gamble (ii)?

(a) Suppose the utility function is a general concave function u. Will the investor ever prefer or be indifferent between the status quo and the fair gamble, gain or lose a with equal probability?

(b) What happens if u is strictly concave or convex?

[**B6**] Prove that each of following utility functions is strictly concave and non-decreasing on suitably restricted domains of w.

(a) $\log(w + w_0)$, where $w_0 > 0$;
(b) $(w + w_0)^\alpha$, where $w_0 > 0$ and $< \alpha < 1$;
(c) $w - \beta w^2, \beta > 0$;
(d) $-e^{-\delta w}, \delta > 0$.

[**B7**] *St. Petersburg Paradox*

Consider a gamble where a fair coin is repeatedly tossed until a head is obtained. If a head is obtained on the first toss, the payoff is $2, $4 if the head is obtained on the second toss, $8 on the third, and so on, so that with each additional toss the payoff doubles.

(a) Show that the expected return from this gamble is infinite.

(b) Let x be the amount that one is willing to pay for the gamble. What is the probability that a profit is made if $x = 10, 20, 50, 100, 1,000$?

(c) What would you be willing to pay for the gamble? Explain the St. Petersburg paradox.

(d) Illustrate how the paradox may be resolved by choosing a particular concave utility function (such as $\log(w)$ or $w^{1/2}$, where w is wealth) and by showing that there exists an optimal value of the gamble at all (finite) initial wealth levels.

(e) Show that it is always possible to create a gamble that leads to a paradox if the gambler's utility function is unbounded.

[**B8**] The preference ordering of an investor generally depends on his wealth level w.

(a) Show that if the utility functions $u(w)$ and $u(w + \beta)$ represent the same preference ordering for all values of β, then these utility functions satisfy

$$u(w + \beta) = a(\beta)u(w) + b(\beta),$$

where the constants a and b may depend on β.

(b) Show that the only utility functions that have the property that their preference orderings are independent of wealth are $u(w) = aw$ or $u(w) = be^{cw}$ where a, b and c are real numbers. [Hint: Differentiate the equation in (a) with respect to w and β, combine these, and solve the resulting differential equation with $da(\beta)/d\beta = $ or $\neq 0$.]

[**B9**] Suppose that an investor's utility function is $u(w) = w^3$.

(a) An investor can take a gamble on a risky asset and/or purchase insurance to cover risk below a fixed level. Construct a fair gamble, an actuarially unfair insurance situation, and a wealth level for which the investor simultaneously wishes to gamble and purchase insurance.

   For the example used in (a), show that at different wealth levels the investor is

(b) unwilling to purchase the given insurance, and

(c) unwilling to take the given gamble.

(d) Is there a wealth level at which the investor is unwilling to purchase the given insurance or to take the given gamble?

(e) Is the result of (d) general in the sense that its answer remains the same for all gambles that illustrate (a)?

Illustrate the wealth ranges and sets of gambles for which the investor is

(f) a risk averter, or
(g) a risk taker.

[B10] Suppose that an investor's preference ordering for proportional gambles on wealth is independent of his wealth level.

(a) Show that

$$p_1 u[w(1 + r_1)] + p_2 u[w(1 + r_2)]$$
$$= q_1 u[w(1 + s_1)] + q_2 u[w(1 + s_2)],$$

if and only if

$$p_1 u(1 + r_1) + p_2 u(1 + r_2) = q_1 u(1 + s_1) + q_2 u(1 + s_2),$$
$$\text{with } w > 0, \ p_i, q_i > 0, \ p_1 + p_2 = q_1 + q_2 = 1.$$

(b) Show that u must have the form w^α or $\log(w)$.

[B11] Let c be the cost of a lottery ticket or an insurance policy and r_c the opportunity rate on c. Suppose that the possible monetary outcomes are $\xi_1, \ldots, \xi_m$ having probabilities $p_i > 0$ and that the opportunity interest rate on each ξ_i is r_i. Over a T-period horizon the augmented cost is $c_\alpha = c(1 + r_c)^T$ and the expected augmented gain (or loss) is $y_\alpha = \sum_i \xi_i p_i (1 + r_i)^T$. Under the suggested approach, choices under uncertainty are dictated by the relative sizes of c_α and y_α.

(a) When does this approach reduce to the expected utility approach?
(b) Show that a gamble is fair if $c = \sum p_i \xi_i$.
(c) Show that for fair gambles if

$$r_i \gtreqless r_c \quad \text{for all } i, \quad \text{then } y_\alpha \gtreqless c_\alpha.$$

(d) What can you conclude from (c)? What can be said if $r_i > r_c$ and $r_j < r_c$?

(e) Show that an augmented income maximizer will prefer a ticket in a fair lottery over the sure income c if lending rates are increasing functions of the amount lent — assuming that each $\xi_i > c > 0$, except ξ_n, which is zero.

(f) Suppose that borrowing rates are increasing functions of the amount borrowed. Suppose further that in the fair insurance case the investor is able to pay for the premium without outside borrowing but will have to borrow if adverse outcomes occur without insurance. Show that it is optimal to purchase insurance as long as the lending rate is less than the borrowing rate.

(g) Show that the augmented income approach can explain the phenomenon of simultaneous insurance and gambling activities.

[B12] Suppose an investor has a monotone, non-decreasing, differentiable, concave utility function $u(w)$ over wealth w. Assume further that $w \geq 0$. We are concerned with the question of when the expected utility will be finite, given that u may be unbounded.

(a) Suppose $u'(0)$ and $E(w)$ are finite. Show that expected utility is finite. [Hint: First establish that $u'(w)$ is uniformly bounded, then utilize the differential definition of a concave function.]

It is appropriate to consider weakening the assumptions on the finiteness of marginal utility at zero wealth and/or the finiteness of the mean wealth level.

(b) Suppose u is a polynomial of degree n. Show that expected utility is never finite if $E(w)$ is infinite. [Hint: Begin by showing that if $E(w)$ is infinite, then so is $E(w'')$ for all $n > 1$.]

(c) Show that the result in (b) also holds for any non-constant, monotone, non-decreasing, concave utility function. Hence it is not possible to relax the assumption concerning the finiteness of the mean vector.

(d) Suppose that $E(w)$ is finite and $u(0)$ is finite with no specification regarding the finiteness of $u'(0)$ and $u(w_0)$ is finite for some $w_0 > 0$. Show that expected utility is finite.

(e) Extend the result in (d) to the case $w \geq A$ for some $A > -\infty$.

[B13] It is given that

$$\int_{y}^{0} [G(x) - F(x)]dx \geq 0 \quad \text{for all } y < 0,$$

and

$$\int_{0}^{y} [G(x) - F(x)]dx \geq 0 \quad \text{for all } y > 0.$$

We conclude that,

(a) F dominates G by PSD, i.e., for all S-shape preferences.
(b) F dominates G by MSD, i.e., for all reverse S-shape preferences.

Which of the above statements is true? Discuss.

[B14] F and G are given by the following distributions:

G		F	
Outcome	Probability	Outcome	Probability
-10	$1/4$	-12	$1/4$
-2	$1/4$	0	$1/4$
$+10$	$1/4$	$+15$	$1/2$
$+20$	$1/4$		

Draw the two cumulative distributions and determine if there is FSD, SSD, PSD or MSD.

[B15] The returns on two investments are related by $y = 2x$ where x and y stand for the returns on the two investments under consideration.

(a) Is there FSD? SSD? PSD? MSD? Demonstrate your answer by constructing a numerical example.

(b) Repeat question (a) above given that $x > 0$ and $y > 0$.

(c) Repeat question (a) above given that $x < 0$ and $y < 0$.

[B16] Consider a two-period problem with consumption stream (c_1, c_2). Given the utility function $u(c)$, define the intertemporal utility $V(c_1, c_2) = u(c_1) + u(c_2)$.

(a) If $u(c) = \frac{c^{1-\gamma}}{1-\gamma}$. $\gamma < 1$, then show that smooth/constant consumption is preferable.

(b) For consumption (c_1, c_2), let the intertemporal utility be

$$V(c_1, c_2) = [c_1^\rho + \beta c_2^\rho]^{\frac{1}{\rho}}, 0 \neq \rho < 1, 0 < \beta < 1.$$

Describe the effect of the risk parameter ρ and substitution parameter β on consumption.

(c) For consumption (c_1, C_2), where C_2 is random, let the intertemporal utility be $V(c_1, C_2) = W(c_1, \mu(C_2))$, where μ is the certainty equivalent and $W(c, z) = [c^\rho + \beta z^\rho]^{\frac{1}{\rho}}$, $0 \neq \rho < 1, 0 < \beta < 1$.
Describe the effects of the parameters.

Exercise Source Notes

Exercise [B3] is adapted from problem 1, p. 57 in Ziemba–Vickson (1975). Exercise [B5] is adapted from problem 2, p. 57 in Ziemba–Vickson. Exercise [B6] is adapted from problem 3, p. 57 in Ziemba–Vickson. Exercise [B7] is adapted from problem 4, p. 57 in

Ziemba–Vickson. Exercise [B8] is adapted from problem 5, p. 57 in Ziemba–Vickson. Exercise [B9] is adapted from problem 6, p. 57 in Ziemba–Vickson. Exercise [B11] is adapted from problem 18, p. 61 in Ziemba–Vickson. Exercise [B12] is adapted from problem 32, p. 364 in Ziemba–Vickson. Exercises [B13], [B14] and [15] were provided by H. Levy to illustrate stochastic dominance.

SECTION C: STOCHASTIC DOMINANCE

The ordering of individual preferences with a utility or value functional is dependent on the chosen utility. There are important almost canonical utilities. Bernoulli (1738) provided a rationale for log utility, which together with the broader class of power utilities, has been useful in analyzing problems in decision making under uncertainty. Log utility is the basis of the golden rule of investing or Fortunes Formula, the Kelly (1956) strategy, which maximizes the asymptotic rate of capital growth. However, as indicated in Section B, there is some indeterminacy over individual utilities in practice and even over classes of utilities which reflect consistent preference attitudes.

In the problem of financial decision making, the accumulated capital from investing in risky assets is a random variable. The preference for random variables can be expressed in terms of the characteristics of their distributions with the order relations of stochastic dominance. So first order stochastic dominance (FSD) is characterized by the cumulative distributions:

> Let X_1 and X_2 be random variables with distribution functions F_1 and F_2, respectively. Then X_1 FSD X_2 iff $F_1(x) \leq F_2(x), \forall x$. Alternatively, X_1 FSD X_2 iff $F_1^{-1}(p) \geq F_2^{-1}(p), 0 \leq p \leq 1$.

In most cases the distribution functions would not be ordered, but would rather intersect at various values of x. A reasonable approach to intersecting distributions is to consider the area between them.

If the intersection(s) is such that the in accumulating area the positive is not offset by the negative, then second order stochastic dominance (SSD) holds:

> Let X_1 and X_2 be random variables with distribution functions F_1 and F_2, respectively. Then X_1 SSD X_2 iff $\int_{-\infty}^{y} F_1(x)dx \le \int_{-\infty}^{y} F_2(x)dx, \forall y$. Alternatively, X_1 SSD X_2 iff $\int_0^\alpha F_1^{-1}(p)dp \ge \int_0^\alpha F_2^{-1}(p), 0 \le \alpha \le 1$.

Hadar and Russell (1969) discuss first and second order stochastic dominance for bounded random variables. Obviously FSD implies SSD. The mean of a random variable in terms of its inverse distribution is $\mu = \int_0^1 F^{-1}(p)dp$. The calculation $\int_0^\alpha F^{-1}(p)dp = L(\alpha)$ defines the incomplete mean, and the graph $\{(\alpha, L(\alpha), 0 \le \alpha \le 1\}$ is called the absolute Lorenz curve (Lorenz, 1905). SSD is based on an ordering of Lorenz curves. As with the distribution functions, it is possible that the Lorenz curves intersect and the random variables cannot be ordered. Dominated and undominated curves $(X(p) = F^{-1}(p) - \text{distribution}, L(p) - \text{Lorenz})$ are shown in Fig. 1.

The integration process can be continued with the calculation of the cumulative area between the curves to get higher orders of dominance. The dominance becomes weaker, but more random variables are ordered by higher orders.

> Let X_1 and X_2 be random variables with distribution functions F_1 and F_2, respectively. The kth degree

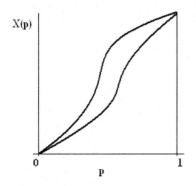
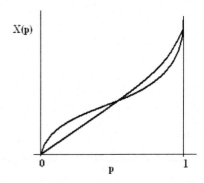

Fig. 1(a):   FSD.

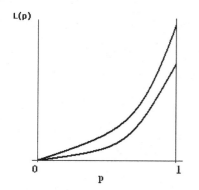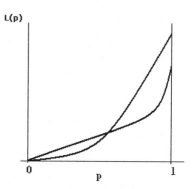

Fig. 1(b): SSD.

ordering of X_1 and X_2 is $X_1 \succcurlyeq_k X_2$, where

$$\int\limits_{0}^{\alpha} \cdots \left\{ \int\limits_{0}^{p_3} \left\{ \int\limits_{0}^{p_2} [F_1^{-1}(p_1) - F_2^{-1}(p_1)]dp_1 \right\} dp_2 \right\} \cdots dp_{k-1} \geq 0,$$

for all $\alpha \in (0,1]$.

A lower order implies all subsequent orders, but the reverse is not true.

The ordering defined by stochastic dominance is linked to the preference relation from expected utility. In that way, stochastic dominance from distributions feeds into the expected utility theory approach to financial decision making under uncertainty. Hanoch and Levy (1969) show that stochastic dominance can be defined by classes of utilities as characterized by higher order derivatives of the utility, with $u^{(k)}$ being the kth derivative. Consider the class of utilities $U_k = \{u|(-1)^{j-1}u^{(j)} \geq 0, j = 1, \ldots, k\}$. So U_1 is the class of monotone non-decreasing functions, U_2 is the class of monotone non-decreasing, concave functions and so on.

(i) Let X_1 and X_2 be random variables with distribution functions F_1 and F_2, respectively. Then X_1 FSD X_2 iff either

$$F_1^{-1}(p) \geq F_2^{-1}(p), \ 0 \leq p \leq 1,$$

or

$$Eu(X_1) \geq Eu(X_2) \text{ for all } u \in U_1.$$

(ii) Let X_1 and X_2 be random variables with distribution functions F_1 and F_2, respectively. Then X_1 SSD X_2 iff either

$$\int_0^\alpha F_1^{-1}(p)dp \geq \int_0^\alpha F_2^{-1}(p), \ 0 \leq \alpha \leq 1,$$

or

$$Eu(X_1) \geq Eu(X_2) \text{ for all } u \in U_2.$$

(iii) Let X_1 and X_2 be random variables with distribution functions F_1 and F_2, respectively. Then X_1 KSD $X_2, X_1 \succcurlyeq_k X_2$, iff either

$$\int_0^\alpha \cdots \left\{ \int_0^{p_3} \left\{ \int_0^{p_2} [F_1^{-1}(p_1) - F_2^{-1}(p_1)]dp_1 \right\} dp_2 \right\} \cdots dp_{k-1} \geq 0$$

$$\text{for all } \alpha \in (0,1],$$

or

$$Eu(X_1) \geq Eu(X_2) \text{ for all } u \in U_k.$$

With second order dominance, the distributions can cross many times as long as the order in area between the distributions is maintained. For distributions which cross just once, second order dominance depends on the means: If $F_1(x) \leq F_2(x), x < x_0$ and $F_1(x) \geq F_2(x), x \geq x_0$, then X_1 SSD $X_2 \Leftrightarrow E(X_1) \geq E(X_2)$ (Hammond, 1973).

In certain cases second order dominance is characterized by the first two moments of the distributions (Fishburn, 1980). Let X_1 and X_2 be random variables with distribution functions F_1 and F_2, and (means, variances) given by $(\mu_{X_1}, \sigma_{X_1}^2)$ and $(\mu_{X_2}, \sigma_{X_2}^2)$, respectively. Let $\mu_{X_1} > \mu_{X_2}$ and assume

$$F_1(x_1) = F_2(x_2) \text{ for all } x_1, x_2 \text{ such that}$$

$$\frac{x_1 - \mu_{X_1}}{\sigma_{X_1}} = \frac{x_2 - \mu_{X_2}}{\sigma_{X_2}},$$

$$F_1(x^*) > F_2(x^*) \text{ for some } x^*.$$

Then X_1 SSD X_2 iff $\sigma_{X_1}^2 \leq \sigma_{X_2}^2$.

The higher orders of stochastic dominance can be continued with the classes of utilities based on derivatives of the utility function. So X_1 kth order dominates X_2 iff $Eu(X_1) \geq Eu(X_2)$ for all $u \in U_k$. Again the higher order dominance is weaker, but an interesting class of utilities arises when $k \to \infty$. The sign of successive derivatives alternate, which characterizes the class of power utilities: $\{u_\alpha(x) = \frac{1}{\alpha}x^\alpha, \alpha < 1\}$. The special member of this class is the log utility, when $\alpha \to 0$, which is the utility of Bernoulli (1738), and it dominates other power utilities in the sense that maximizing log of terminal wealth gives the maximal growth rate of capital.

The dominance described above is for a single period, usually the final period of accumulated capital. However, the capital is accumulated from investments over time and the trajectory to final wealth could be important in the assessment of utility. Levy (1973), Levy and Paroush (1974) extend the notions of stochastic dominance to the multi-period case. (See also Huang *et al.* (1978).) Two situations are discussed. In one case the intertemporal utility is assumed to be additive, so that for the multi-period capital stream $(x_1, \ldots, x_T)$ the utility is $u(x_1, \ldots, x_T) = \sum_{t=1}^{T} u_t(x_t)$.

Consider multi-period capital streams $X = (X, \ldots, X_T)$ and $Y = (Y_1, \ldots, Y_T)$, with multivariate distributions $F(X)$ and $G(Y)$. Let F_t and G_t be the marginal distributions for period $t, t = 1, \ldots, T$. Then necessary and sufficient conditions for X *FSD* Y are $F_t(w) \leq G_t(w), \forall w$, $t = 1, \ldots, T$.

So in the case of additive utility, the ordering of marginal distributions allows the stochastic dominance result to extend to multiple periods. This result does not require temporal independence. The second order (and higher order) dominance would follow by considering the area between (integration) for marginal distributions.

A second case considered by Levy and Paroush involves the geometric process where the final return is the product of period returns: $W(X) = X_1 \times \cdots \times X_T$. So each period provides a rate of return. The utility is for the final wealth $u(W)$.

Consider the multi-period return streams $X = (X_1, \ldots, X_T)$ and $Y = (Y_1, \ldots, Y_T)$ with multivariate distributions $F(X)$ and $G(Y)$. Then necessary conditions for $W(X)$ FSD $W(Y)$ are

(i) $F_{t|t-1,\ldots,1}(x_t|x_{t-1}, \ldots, x_1) \leq G_{t|t-1,\ldots,1}(x_t|x_{t-1}, \ldots, x_1)$
     $t = 1, \ldots, T$ where $F_{t|t-1,\ldots,1}$ is the conditional distribution at time t, and

(ii) The conditional distribution $F_{t|t-1,\ldots,1}(\cdot|x_{t-1}, \ldots, x_1)$
     is non-decreasing in $x_{t-1}, \ldots, x_1$.

This is a very common situation, where the terminal wealth is evaluated but the returns by period are serially correlated. The condition is necessary but not sufficient.

Stochastic dominance is a partial order. Suppose that second order dominance is the relation of interest since it incorporates risk aversion through concave utilities. If efficient distributions are undominated, then efficient investment strategies (portfolios) are ones whose wealth at a specified time (horizon) is undominated. Dybvig and Ross (1985) put this in terms of utility functions in a class, such as U_k.

If $X_T(\lambda)$ is the wealth at time T from an investment strategy λ in the feasible set of strategies Λ, then $X_T(\lambda^*)$ is kth order efficient if there exists a utility $u \in U_k$ such that

$$Eu(X_T(\lambda^*)) = \max_{\lambda \in \Lambda} Eu(X_T(\lambda)).$$

Efficiency applies to any order of stochastic dominance, although risk aversion and SSD are standard. The set of efficient strategies (portfolios) is characterized by stochastic dominance, but is difficult to calculate. The special case of normally distributed random variables is tractable and has received a lot of attention.

Let X_1 and X_2 be normally distributed random variables with means μ_1, μ_2 and variances σ_1^2, σ_2^2, respectively. Then the following are equivalent

  (i) $Eu(X_1) \geq Eu(X_2)$ for any utility $u \in U_2$.
  (ii) $\mu_1 \geq \mu_1$ and $\sigma_1^2 \leq \sigma_2^2$.

Second order dominance and efficiency are determined by the parameters in the normal distribution. Markowitz (1952) originated the concept of mean-variance efficiency and it has been a cornerstone of portfolio theory. The set of MV efficient points, called the efficient frontier, are determined from the problem for each mean μ_0,

$$P(\mu_0): \min_{\lambda}\{\sigma^2(X(\lambda))|\mu(\lambda) \geq \mu_0, \lambda \ feasible\}.$$

Markowitz's (μ, σ^2) criterion is neither necessary nor sufficient for second order dominance in general, as additional conditions on the distribution are required. Tobin (1958) claimed that the mean versus variance analysis is applicable in two cases:

  (a) When the utility function is quadratic;
  (b) When the distributions of the portfolios are all members of a two parameter family.

    ■ The actual requirement is that the distributions need to be members of a two parameter family, with parameters being independent non-decreasing functions of μ and σ^2.

The log-normal distribution $X \propto LN(\mu, \sigma^2)$ is a two parameter distribution, but the mean and variance of the log-normal are dependent functions of (μ, σ^2).

Samuelson (1970) considered the situation where the mean and variance are approximately sufficient for portfolio analysis.

(c) When the distributions of the portfolios are members of a "compact" family, where the moments of order three and higher are small relative to the first two moments.

If the planning horizon is short, then this "compact" condition is valid. The convergence to "compactness" as the planning horizon decreases is formally developed in Ohlson (1975).

Rothschild and Stiglitz (1970) consider four characterizations of stochastic dominance involving means and variances.

1. $X_2 \triangleq X_1 + Z$, where $\triangleq$ means has the same distribution, and $E[Z|X_1] = 0$, almost surely, Z independent of X_1. So $\mu_{X_1} = \mu_{X_2}$, and X_1 SSD X_2. Of course, by construction $\sigma^2_{X_2} > \sigma^2_{X_1}$.

2. $Eu(X_1) \geq Eu(X_2), \forall$ concave $u, \mu_{X_1} = \mu_{X_2}$.

3. X_2 has more weight in the tails than X_1, where $\mu_{X_1} = \mu_{X_2}$.

4. $\sigma^2_{X_2} > \sigma^2_{X_1}$ and $\mu_{X_1} = \mu_{X_2}$.

They show that (1), (2) and (3) are equivalent, but (4) is neither necessary nor sufficient for SSD. This result was also discovered by Blackwell and Girshick (1954) and earlier by Hardy, Littlewood and Polya (1934).

Diamond and Stiglitz (1974) considered the effect of riskiness (variability, heavier tails) on the efficient solution. Consider the problem for scalar valued X,

$$\max_{X \in K} E_\xi u(\xi, X) dF(\xi).$$

Assuming an interior optimal solution, the optimal solution X^* satisfies

$$\int \frac{\partial u(\xi, X)}{\partial X} dF(\xi) = 0.$$

If $\frac{\partial u(\xi, X)}{\partial X}$ is a concave (convex) function of ξ, then an increase/decrease in riskiness will decrease/increase X^*.

In addition to mean-variance efficiency, the other tractable case of efficiency follows from the negative power utilities. The negative power efficient points are defined as: $X_\alpha = argmax\{u_\alpha(X)\}$ for some α. If the distribution of portfolio returns is log-normal the negative power efficient points have the form $X_\alpha = \frac{1}{1-\alpha}X^*$, where $X^* = argmax\{\ln(X)\}$. This class of strategies has generated a lot of interest. X^* is the optimal growth or Kelly strategy, and X_α is fractional Kelly. Many good and bad properties of this strategy and results are reported in MacLean *et al.* (2010).

Prospect and Markowitz Stochastic Dominance: a utility function is *S-shaped* if: there is an inflection point at $x = 0$; $u' \geq 0$ for all $x \neq 0$; $u'' \geq 0$ for $x < 0$ and $u'' \leq 0$ for $x \geq 0$. A *reverse S-shaped* utility has an inflection point at $x = 0$; $u' \geq 0$ for all $x \neq 0$; $u'' \leq 0$ for $x < 0$ and $u'' \geq 0$ for $x > 0$.

Prospect Stochastic Dominance (PSD): Let X_1 and X_2 be random variables with distribution functions F_1 and F_2 respectively.

Then X_1, PSD X_2 *S-shaped* utilities iff:

(i) $\int_x^0 [F_2(t) - F_1(t)]dt \geq 0$ for all $x \leq 0$

(ii) $\int_0^x [F_2(t) - F_1(t)]dt \geq 0$ for all $x \geq 0$.

Markowitz Stochastic Dominance (MSD): X_1 MSD X_2 for all reverse S-shaped utilities iff:

(i) $\int_{-\infty}^x [F_2(t) - F_1(t)]dt \geq 0$ for all $x \leq 0$

(ii) $\int_x^\infty [F_2(t) - F_1(t)]dt \geq 0$ for all $x \geq 0$.

A detailed treatment of the various stochastic dominance relations is provided in Sriboonchitta *et al.* (2010).

Readings

Bernoulli, D. (1738). Exposition on a new theory of the measurement of risk (translated by L. Sommer in 1954), *Econometrica* **22**: 23–36. (Reprinted in *The Kelly Capital Growth Investment Criterion*, MacLean, L. Thorp, E. O., and Ziemba, W. T. (eds.), Singapore: World Scientific Press, 2010.)

Blackwell, D. and Girshick, M. A. (1954). *Theory of Games and Statistical Decisions.* Wiley: New York.

Diamond, P. and Stiglitz, J. (1974). Increases in risk and risk aversion, *Journal of Economic Theory* **8**: 337–360.

Dybvig, P. and Ross, S. (1985). Differential information and performance measurement using a security market line, *Journal of Finance* **40**(2): 383–399.

Fishburn, P. (1980). Stochastic dominance and moments of distributions, *Mathematics of Operations Research* **5**, 94–100.

Hammond, J. (1973). Simplifying choice between uncertain prospects where preference is nonlinear, *Management Science* **20**: 1047–1072.

Hanoch, G. and Levy, H. (1969). The efficiency analysis of choices involving risk, *Review of Economic Studies* **36**(3): 335–346.

Hadar, J. and Russell, W. (1969). Rules for ordering uncertain prospects, *American Economic Review* **59**: 25–33.

Hardy, G. H., Littlewood, J. E. and Polya G. (1933). *Inequalities.* Cambridge: Cambridge University Press.

Huang, C. C., Vertinsky, I. and Ziemba, W. T. (1978). On multiperiod stochastic dominance, *Journal of Financial and Quantitative Analysis* **XIII**: 1–13.

Kelly, J. R. (1956). A new interpretation of the information rate, *Bell System Technical Journal* **35**: 917–926.

Levy, H. (1973). Stochastic dominance, efficiency criteria, and efficient portfolios: The multi-period case (1973), *American Economic Review* **63**(5): 986–994.

Levy, H. and Paroush, J. (1974). Multi-period stochastic dominance, *Management Science* **21**(4): 428–435.

Lorenz, M. O. (1905). Methods of measuring concentration of wealth, *Journal of American Statistical Association* **9**: 209–219.

MacLean, L. C., Thorp, E. O. and Ziemba, W. T. (2010). Long term capital growth: The good and bad properties of the Kelly and fractional Kelly capital growth criterion, *Quantitative Finance* **10**(7): 681–687.

Markowitz, H. (1952). Portfolio Selection, *Journal of Finance* **7**: 77–91.

Ohlson, J. A. (1975). The asymptotic validity of quadratic utility as the trading interval approaches zero, in *Stochastic Optimization Models in Finance*, W. T. Ziemba and R. G. Vickson (eds.), San Diego: Academic Press, 221–234.

Rothschild, M. and Stiglitz, J. E. (1970). Increasing risk I: A definition, *Journal of Economic Theory* **2**(3): 225–243.

Samuelson, P. A. (1970). The fundamental approximation theorem of portfolio analysis in terms of means, variances, ad higher moments, *Review of Economic Studies* **37**: 537–542.

Sriboonchitta, S., Wong, W. K., Dhompongsa, S. and Nguyen, H. T. (2010). *Stochastic Dominance and Applications to Finance, Risk and Economics.* BocaRaton: CRC Press.

Tobin, J. (1958). Liquidity preference as behavior towards risk, *Review of Economic Studies* **25**, 65–86.

Appendix C: Probability and Random Variables

The basis of uncertainty modeling is a probability space (Ω, B, P), where Ω is the sample space, B is a $\sigma-$ field of measurable subsets of Ω, and P is a probability measure. P is a mapping onto $[0, 1]$, with $P(\Omega) = 1$.

Random variables and distributions

A random variable is a function from Ω to the real line $\mathcal{R}$, such that $X^{-1}(A) = \{\omega \in \Omega | X(\omega) \in A\} \in B$, for any Borel set $A \subseteq \mathcal{R}$. So $P_X(A) = P(X^{-1}(A)) = P\{\omega | X(\omega) \in A\}$.

The function $F_X \colon \mathcal{R} \to [0, 1]$, where $F_X(x) = P_X((-\infty, x])$, is called the distribution function of X. F_X is monotone non-decreasing and right continuous, with $\lim_{x \to -\infty} F_{X(x)} = 0$ and $\lim_{x \to -\infty} F_{X(x)} = 1$.

The function $f_X(x) = \frac{d}{dx} F_X(x)$ is the density for X. $f_X(x)dx = dF_X(x)$ is a Lebesque–Stieltjes measure on the Borel subsets of $\mathcal{R}$.

If $X = (X_1, \ldots, X_p)'$ is a vector of random variables, the joint distribution is a function $F \colon \mathcal{R}^p \to [0, 1]$, where

$$F(x_1, \ldots, x_p) = P(X_1 \leq x_1, \ldots, X_p \leq x_p) = P_X\left(\prod_{i=1}^p (-\infty, x_i]\right).$$

P_X is a probability measure on the Borel subsets of $\mathcal{R}^p$. The joint probability density for X is

$$f(x_1, \ldots, x_p) = \frac{\partial^p F(x_1, \ldots, x_p)}{\partial x_1, \ldots, \partial x_p}.$$

The marginal density for X_i is

$$f_i(x_i) = \int_{\mathcal{R}^{p-1}} f(x_1, \ldots, x_p) \partial x_1 \ldots \partial x_{i-1} \partial x_{i+1} \ldots \partial x_p.$$

Moments

A probability distribution may be characterized by its *moments*. The rth moment of x about some fixed point x_0 is defined as the expectation value of $(x - x_0)^r$ where r is an integer.

The mean is the first moment about zero,

$$\mu = E[X] = \int x f(x) dx.$$

The variance is the second moment about the mean (also known as the *second central moment*),

$$\sigma^2 = E[(X - \mu)^2] = \int (x - \mu)^2 f(x) dx.$$

The square root of the variance is the *standard deviation*.

The moments characterize a distribution. The normal distribution is expressed in terms of μ and σ^2. If the raw moments about zero are $E[X^n]$, $n = 0, 1, \ldots$, then the probability density for X can be expressed in terms of the raw moments as

$$f(x) = \sum_{n=0}^{\infty} \left(\int_{-\infty}^{\infty} \frac{(-i2\pi s)^n}{n!} e^{i2\pi x s} ds \right) E[X^n].$$

For the vector of random variables $X = (X_1, \ldots, X_p)'$, the mean is $\mu = (\mu_1, \ldots, \mu_p)'$ and the variance–covariance matrix is

$$\Sigma = \begin{pmatrix} \sigma_1^2 & \cdots & \sigma_{1p} \\ \vdots & \ddots & \vdots \\ \sigma_{p1} & \cdots & \sigma_p^2 \end{pmatrix}, \text{ where } \sigma_{ij} = E(X_i - \mu_i)(X_j - \mu_j).$$

Quantiles

The quantile function (inverse distribution) for a random variable X is defined as

$$F^{-1}(\alpha) = \inf\{x | F(x) \geq \alpha\}, \alpha \in (0, 1].$$

F^{-1} is increasing and left continuous. For distributions F and G, $F(x) \geq G(x), \forall x \in \mathcal{R}$ iff $G^{-1}(p) \geq F^{-1}(p), \forall p \in (0, 1)$.

Lorenz curve

SSD is characterized by the Lorenz curve, which has a long tradition in economics. Lorenz Stochastic Dominance (LSD) is defined by the Absolute Lorenz Curve: $\mathcal{L}(\alpha) = \int_0^\alpha F^{-1}(p)dp, \alpha \in (0,1]$. So $X_1 LSD X_2$ iff $\mathcal{L}_{X_1}(\alpha) \geq \mathcal{L}_{X_2}(\alpha), \alpha \in (0,1)$. $\mathcal{L}(\alpha)$ is increasing and convex with $\mathcal{L}(1) = \mu$.

Gini coefficient

The curvature in the Lorenz curve is determined by the shape of the distribution for a random variable. The curvature determines the area under the curve, so consider $\int_0^1 \mathcal{L}(\alpha)d\alpha = \int_{-\infty}^\infty [\int_{-\infty}^v (x-v)dF(x)]dF(v)$. $[\int_{-\infty}^v (x-v)dF(x)]$ is a measure of variation, particularly in the tails. If the scale is removed to get the Relative Lorenz Curve: $\tilde{\mathcal{L}}(\alpha) = \frac{1}{\mu}L(\alpha)$, then a standardized measure of variation is the Gini Index

$$\varphi(F) = 2 \int\limits_0^1 [\alpha - \tilde{\mathcal{L}}(\alpha)]d\alpha.$$

The Gini is commonly used as a measure of concentration (flip side of variation), with extremes:

$\varphi(F) = 0$ *if* $\tilde{\mathcal{L}}(\alpha) = \alpha$ (uniform distribution),
$\varphi(F) = 1$ *if* $\tilde{\mathcal{L}}(\alpha) = 0, 0 \leq \alpha < 1, \tilde{\mathcal{L}}(1) = 1$ (Atomic distribution).

Section C Exercises

[C1] Consider the random variables X_1 and X_2, with $E(X_1) = E(X_2)$. If $X_1 SSD X_2$, show that Variance$(X_1) \leq$ Variance(X_2).

[C2] Let $VaR_X(\alpha) = F_X^{-1}(\alpha), \alpha \in (0,1)$. Prove that $X_1 FSD X_2$ if and only if $VaR_{X_1}(\alpha) \leq VaR_{X_2}(\alpha), \alpha \in (0.1)$.

[C3] For a random variable X, with distribution F_X, the absolute Lorenz curve is $\mathcal{L}_X(\alpha) = \int_0^\alpha F_X^{-1}(p)dp$. Compute the Lorenz curve for $X \sim N(\mu, \sigma^2)$.

[C4] LSD of X_1 over X_2 holds if $\mathcal{L}_{X_1}(\alpha) \geq L_{X_2}(\alpha), 0 \leq \alpha \leq 1$. Show that LSD is equivalent to SSD.

[C5] Let $X' = (X_1, X_2, \ldots, X_n)$ be i.i.d. returns and consider portfolio weights $w'_n = (1/n, 1/n, \ldots, 1/n)$ and $w' = (w_1, w_2, \ldots, w_n)$, where $0 \leq w_i \leq 1, \sum w_i = 1$. Show that $w'_n X \, SSD \, w'X$.

[C6] Consider random variables X_1 and X_2. Relative to a benchmark b, let $X^+ = \max\{X - b, 0\}$ be the gains and $X^- = \min\{0, X - b\}$ be the losses. Define the S-shaped utility $Eu(X) = Ev_1(X^+) + Ev_2(X^-)$, where $v_1(0) = v_2(0)$ and v_1 concave, v_2 convex. Let PSD denote prospect stochastic dominance. Prove that:
$X_1 \, PSD \, X_2$ iff $Eu(X_1) \geq Eu(X_2)$ for a ll S-shaped utilities.

[C7] Consider random variables X_1 and X_2. Relative to a benchmark b, let $X^+ = \max\{X - b, 0\}$ be the gains and $X^- = \min\{0, X - b\}$ be the losses. Define the reverse S-shaped utility $Eu(X) = Ev_1(X^+) + Ev_2(X^-)$, where $v_1(0) = v_2(0)$ and v_1 convex, v_2 concave. Prove that:
$X_1 \, PSD \, X_2$ iff $Eu(X_1) \geq Eu(X_2)$ for all reverse S-shaped utilities.

[C8] Consider the returns on two stocks in the following table.

Stock 1		Stock 2	
Return	Prob	Return	Prob
$-1,600$	0.25	$-1,000$	0.25
-200	0.25	-800	0.25
1,200	0.25	800	0.25
1,600	0.25	2,000	0.25

(a) Using the definition of S-shaped utility, order the stocks based on Prospect stochastic dominance

(b) Using the definition of reverse S-shaped utility, order the
stocks based on Markowitz stochastic dominance

[C9] Consider the following five investment options

A		B		C		D		E	
Pr	Ret	Pr	Ret	Pr	Ret	Pr	Ret	Pr	Ret
1/2	110	1/3	110	1/2	105	1/2	112	1/4	106
1/2	120	1/3	115	1/4	106	1/2	120	3/4	140
		1/3	130	1/4	108				

*All returns per $100 investment

(a) Which options comprise the efficient set corresponding to
all monotonic non-decreasing preferences well known as
the FSD efficient set?
(b) Which options are included in the efficient set corresponding to all non-decreasing concave preferences well known
as the SSD efficient set?
(c) Demonstrate your answers to parts (a) and (b) graphically.

[C10] Below are given partial data on the distributions of returns
of two investment portfolios.

Portfolio F		Portfolio G	
Return (%)	Probability	Return (%)	Probability
−20	1/100	−19.5	50/100
10	5/100	10	25/100
.	.	.	.
.	.	.	.
.	.	.	.

(a) Is it possible for F to dominate G by FSD?

(b) Is it possible for F to dominate G by SSD?

(c) Answer parts (a) and (b) assuming that the expected return of G is 10% and that the expected return is F is 15%.

[C11] *Financial Leverage and FSD valuation*: consider two corporations L (*Leveraged* firm) and U (*Unleveraged* firm) identical in all respects, except for their financial structures. Thus the distributions of returns of the two firms are fully correlated. While firm L has debt in its capital structure, firm U finance all its operations only with equity. The earnings before interest and tax (EBIT) of each firm is a random variable denoted by X. The following data describe the two firms and the random variable X:

	Firm L	Firm U
Number of shares of common stock (N)	1,000,000	2,000,000
Long term debt	$10,000,000	0

Distribution of earnings before interest and tax for the two firms:

X	Probability
$2,000,000	0.50
$1,000,000	0.25
$500,000	0.25

The market value of the stock of firm U is $20,000,000, and the interest rate that firm L pays on its debt is 7%.

Modigliani and Miller (M&M) have shown that in the absence of corporate taxes the two firms must have the same share price P regardless of capital structure, i.e., $P_L = P_U$. Denote by Y_U the earnings per share of firm U (a random variable) and by Y_L the earnings per share of firm L (also a random variable).

Show that if $P_L > P_U$, arbitrage possibilities exist such that the investor can switch from firm L to firm U while receiving income which dominates the previous income Y_L by FSD.

Hint: when the returns on the stocks of two firms are fully correlated, arbitrage is equivalent to FSD.

[C12] Suppose that X_1 denotes the distribution of returns in period 1, and X_2 the distribution of returns in period 2. The returns are identical and independent over time (i.i.d.). X_1 and X_2 are given by

$X_1(= X_2)$	
Outcome	Probability
0.9	1/3
1.2	1/3
1.5	1/3

(a) Draw the one period cumulative distribution $F(X_1) = F(X_2)$ and calculate the mean and the variance of the random variables.

(b) Draw the two period distribution $F(X_1 \cdot X_2)$ and calculate the mean and the variance of $X_1 \cdot X_2$.

(c) Is the two-period variance equal to twice the one period variance? Explain.

(d) Suppose that the one period return is normally distributed. Can a risk averter who invests for two periods choose her investments by the mean-variance rule? Explain.

[C13] A one-period investor has to choose one of the following two prospects denoted by F and G:

G		F	
Outcome	Probability	Outcome	Probability
1	1/8	2	1/2
3	7/8	10	1/2

(a) Which prospect dominates the other by FSD?
(b) Which prospect is optimal for the preference $U(x) = a + bx$ $(b > 0)$?
(c) Which prospect is optimal for the preference $U(x) = \log x$?
(d) Assume that the returns are identical and independent over time (i.i.d.). Calculate the two-period distributions of returns.
(e) Draw the one-period and the two-period cumulative distributions. Is there FSD in the two-period case? How do you explain the difference in your answer to (a) and (e)?

[C14] A risk averter investor faces the following two prospects and she has to choose one of them:

G		F	
Outcome	Probability	Outcome	Probability
1	1/8	$\sqrt{3.5}$	1/4
4	7/8	10	3/4

Is there FSD? Is there SSD?

Assuming identical independent random variables (i.i.d.), calculate the two-period distributions of prospects F and G. For the two-period investor, is there FSD? Is there SSD? Draw the two-period distribution of each prospect. Explain your results.

[C15] Efficient sets

(a) "Assuming i.i.d., the multi-period SSD efficient set must be smaller or equal to the one-period SSD efficient set". Is this statement true or false? Explain.

(b) "Assuming i.i.d., the multi-period mean-variance efficient set must be larger or equal to the one-period efficient set". Is this statement true or false? How do you explain the contradiction in the answers of (a) and (b) above? Which assertion is technically true but economically invalid?

[C16] Consider the following return structure:

Outcome	Probability
a	p
1/2	q
1	$1 - p - q$

where p, q and a are given parameters such that $a < \frac{1}{2}, p \geq 0, q \geq 0, p + q = 1$. Suppose for returns Y_1 and Y_2 that $(a, p, q) = (\frac{1}{8}, \frac{7}{16}, \frac{1}{16})$ and $(0, \frac{1}{8}, \frac{3}{4})$, respectively.

(a) Show that $\mu_{Y_1} \leq \mu_{Y_2}, \sigma_{Y_1}^2 \geq \sigma_{Y_2}^2$.

(b) Find a non-decreasing concave utility function such that Y_1 is preferred to Y_2.

(c) Find a non-decreasing concave utility function such that Y_2 is preferred to Y_1.

(d) Interpret the results in (b) and (c).

(e) Suppose a is the same for both Y_1 and Y_2 (but p and q remain as originally specified). Show that Y_2 is preferred to Y_1 for all non-decreasing utility functions.

(f) Find values of p and q such that Y_2 is preferred to Y_1 for all non-decreasing concave utility functions.

[C17] Consider an investor having a quadratic utility for wealth

$$u(w) = 2kw - w^2, k > 0, 0 \le w \le k.$$

Suppose that random investments X_1, X_2, with $0 \le X_1, X_2 \le k$, have means μ_1, μ_2 and variances σ_1^2, σ_2^2, respectively.

(a) Show that X_1 is preferred to X_2, i.e., has higher expected utility, if and only if $2\Delta\mu(k - \bar{\mu}) - \Delta\sigma^2$, where $\Delta\mu = \mu_1 - \mu_2, \bar{\mu} = \frac{1}{2}(\mu_1 + \mu_2), \Delta\sigma^2 = \sigma_1^2 - \sigma_2^2$.

(b) Show that X_1 is preferred to X_2 if $\mu_1 > \mu_2$ and $\sigma_1 < \sigma_2$.

(c) Show that (b) is not necessarily true if the range of X_1 and X_2 is $[0, \infty)$.

(d) Find X_1 and X_2 such that X_1 is preferred to X_2 even though $\mu_1 < \mu_2$.

[C18] Consider an investor having the quadratic utility function of wealth

$$u(w) = 2kw - w^2, k > 0, 0 \le w \le k.$$

We are interested in preference criteria for the dominance of X_1 over X_2 when the only information known is that

(i) $0 \le X_1, X_2 \le k$;

(ii) The means and variances $\mu_1, \mu_2, \sigma_1^2, \sigma_2^2$ are known with $\Delta\mu = \mu_2 - \mu_1 \ge 0$; and X_1 and X_2 have symmetric distributions.

Let R_i be the ranges

$$R_i = \inf\{b - a | P(X_i > b) = P(X_i < a) = 0\}.$$

(a) Show that $R_i \le 2(k - \mu_i)$.

(b) Show that $R_i \ge 2\sigma_i$.

Let $A = \max\{\mu_1 + \sigma_1, \mu_2 + \sigma_2\}$.

(c) Show that X_1 is preferred to X_2 if $2\Delta\mu(A - \bar{\mu}) - \Delta\sigma^2 > 0$.

[C19] Suppose X and Y are random variables taking values in a closed convex subset of the real line. Define Y to be stochastically smaller in mean than X, written $Y \prec X$ if and only if $E(Y - t)^+ \le E(X - t)^+$ for all $t, a^+ = \max(a, 0)$.

(a) Show that $Y \prec X$ if and only if $\int_t^\infty [G(x) - \dot{F}(x)]dx \ge 0$, where F and G are the cumulative distribution functions of X and Y, respectively.

(b) Show that $Y \prec X$ if and only if $Eu(Y) \le Eu(X)$ for all convex non-decreasing utility functions u.

(c) Interpret (b).

(d) Illustrate some problem types for which such utility functions would arise naturally.

(e) (Hanoch–Levy) X is preferred to Y by risk averters, say $Y \ll X$ if $Eu(X) \ge Eu(Y)$ for all concave non-decreasing utility functions u. Under what conditions are the statements $Y \prec X$ and $Y \ll X$ equivalent?

[C20] Let X and Y be discrete random variables concentrated on the finite set of points $\Omega = \{a_1, \ldots, a_n\} \subset [a, b]$ Let X_1, be a discrete random variable concentrated on Ω, and let $p_i = P[X = a_i], p'_i = P[X_1 = a_i], X_1$ is said to differ from X by a mean preserving spread (MPS) if

(i) $p_i = p'_i$ except for four values i_1, i_2, i_3, i_4, with $a_{i_1}, a_{i_2}, a_{i_3}, a_{i_4}$;

(ii) $p'_{i_1} - p_{i_1} = -(p'_{i_2} - p_{i_2}) \ge 0, -(p'_{i_3} - p_{i_3}) = p'_{i_4} - p_{i_4} \ge 0$;

(iii) $\sum_{j=1}^4 a_{i_j}(p'_{i_j} - p_{i_j}) = 0$.

(a) Show that X_1 has less probability mass in the middle and more mass in the tails.

(b) Show that $E(X_1) = E(X)$.

[C21] Let X be a random variable with a cumulative distribution F defined on $[a, b]$. The random variable Y differs from X by a sequence of mean preserving spreads (MPSs) if there exists a finite sequence $X = X_0, X_1, \ldots, X_{N+1} = Y$, such that X_{i+1} differs from X_i by a MPS. Let G be the cumulative distribution of Y. Assume that $EX = EY$, and $\int_a^x [G(y) - F(y)]dy \geq 0$, for all $x \in [a, b]$.

(a) Show that Y differs from X by a sequence of MPSs.

(b) Show there exists a random variable Z such that $P[Y \leq x] = P[X + Z \leq x]$ for all x, with $E[Z|X] = 0$.

[C22] Two random variables X_1 and X_2 are equal in distribution, written as $X_1 \stackrel{\mathrm{m}}{=} X_2$, if $P[X_1 \leq x] = P[X_2 \leq x]$ for all x.

Define two orderings of random variables:

$$Y \prec X \text{ if } Y \stackrel{\mathrm{m}}{=} X + Z, \quad \text{with } E[Z|X] \leq 0,$$
$$Y \prec_0 X \text{ if } Y \stackrel{\mathrm{m}}{=} X + Z, \quad \text{with } E[Z|X] = 0.$$

(a) Show that if $Y \prec X$, then there exists a non-negative function f such that $Y \prec_0 X - f(X)$.

Conversely, if $Y \prec X$, and f is any non-negative function, then $Y \prec X + f(X)$.

(b) Show that if $Eu(X) \geq Eu(Y)$ for all concave non-decreasing u where X and Y are defined on finite ranges, then there exists a non-negative f such that $Eu[X - f(X)] \geq Eu(Y)$.

For all concave u (whether non-decreasing or not).

(c) If X and Y are defined on finite ranges, if $EX = EY$, and if $Eu(X) \geq Eu(Y)$ for all concave non-decreasing u, show that $Eu(X) \geq Eu(Y)$ for all concave u.

[C23] Given that $Eu(X) \geq Eu(Y)$ for all concave non-decreasing u, find an algorithm for constructing a joint distribution function of X and Z such that $E[Z|X] \leq 0$ and $P[Y \leq x] = P[X + Z \leq x]$ for all x.

[C24] (*n*th-order stochastic dominance) Consider the set U_n of utility functions such that

$$U_n = \{u | u^{(k)} \geq 0, k \text{ odd and } u^{(k)} \leq 0, k \text{ even}, k = 1, \ldots, n\},$$

where $u^{(k)}$ denotes the kth derivative of u.

To avoid technical problems consider random variables X and Y with finite range $[a, b]$.

(a) Determine necessary and sufficient conditions for stochastic dominance in U_n, that is, for $Eu(x) \geq Eu(Y)$ for all $u \in U_n$.

(b) Determine necessary and sufficient conditions for stochastic dominance over the set:

$$U_\infty = \{u | u^{(k)} \geq 0, k \text{ odd and } u^{(k)} \leq 0,$$
$$k \text{ even, } k = 1, 2, \ldots\}.$$

Exercise Source Notes

Exercises [C9], [C10], [C11] were provided by H. Levy. Exercise [C16] is adapted from Ziemba–Vickson (1975): p. 173 # 7. Exercise [C17] is adapted from Ziemba–Vickson: p. 172 # 6. Exercise [C18] is adapted from Ziemba–Vickson: p. 172 # 5.

Exercise C[19] is adapted from Ziemba–Vickson: p. 185 # 5. Exercise C[20] is adapted from Ziemba–Vickson: p. 188 # 12. Exercise C[22] is adapted from Ziemba–Vickson: p. 189 # 13. Exercise C[23] is adapted from Ziemba–Vickson: p. 191 # 15. Exercise C[24] is adapted from Ziemba–Vickson: p. 195 # 20.

SECTION D: RISK AVERSION AND STATIC PORTFOLIO THEORY

The components of the financial decision problems are assets, prices, utilities and efficiency. However, there are other important consider- ations in the decision models and the data inputs, which affect the quality of investment decisions in constructing a portfolio.

One significant issue is the computability of an efficient invest- ment strategy. A major advantage of Markowitz' (Markowitz (1952, 1959, 1987) and Markowitz and Van Dijk (2006)) mean-variance anal- ysis is the relative ease of computing optimal strategies and as such it is a practical technique. Ziemba *et al.* (1974) consider the general problem

$$\max Eu(R'x), s.t.e'x = 1, x \in K,$$

where E represents expectation with respect to the uncertainty in $R' = (R_1, \ldots, R_n)$, the vector of risky asset returns. K is a convex set that represents additional constraints on the choice of the investment strategy x. It is assumed that R is joint normal and that Tobin's riskless asset exists, so that borrowing and lending can occur at the risk free rate r.

Ziemba *et al.* propose a two-step approach based on Tobin's (1958) result that the distribution of proportions x^* in the risky assets is independent of the utility function assuming it is concave. So the first step is to find the proportions invested in risky assets using a fractional program:

$$\max_{x} \left\{ \frac{(R - re)'x - r}{(x'\Sigma x)^{\frac{1}{2}}} \middle| e'x = 1, x \in K \right\}.$$

The fractional program always has a unique solution and it may be solved via Lemke's algorithm for the linear complementarity problem or as a quadratic program.

The second step is to determine the optimal ratios of risky to non-risky assets. The return on the risky portfolio is $R^* \sim N(\mu'x^*, x^{*'}\Sigma x^*)$, where (μ, Σ) are the (mean, variance) of R. The optimal mix of R^* and the risk-free asset may be found by solving

$$\max_{-\infty < \alpha \leq 1} Eu(\alpha r + (1 - \alpha)R^*).$$

The second step problem was solved using the quadratic, cubic, exponential, logarithmic, special exponential and power utility functions. The parameters were restricted so that each utility function was strictly increasing and strictly concave for a restricted range of wealth. These utility functions are reasonably diverse in their properties. The quadratic utility produces the mean-variance problem of Markowitz (1952), and the logarithmic utility is the basis of the optimal growth problem introduced by Kelly (1956).

Mean-variance and the analogous two-step procedure use a normality assumption for the distribution of returns on assets. Ziemba (1975) considered the computation of optimal portfolios when returns have a symmetric stable distribution:

$F(y)$ is stable iff for all real numbers $a_1, a_2, 0$, and b_1, b_2, there exists a, b

$$\text{such that the convolution } F\left(\frac{y - b_1}{a_1}\right) *$$

$$F\left(\frac{y - b_2}{a_2}\right) \text{ equals } F\left(\frac{y - b}{a}\right).$$

The normal is a stable distribution when the variance is finite, but the stable family is more general with dispersion replacing variance and has four rather than two parameters. The convolution condition is exactly the requirement for the two-step approach. Based on the two-step procedure, optimal proportions for risky assets are computed, again with a fractional program. A stochastic program finds the optimal mix between the risk-free asset and the random portfolio. The fractional problem is solved for stable distributions. The features needed to use the two-step approach are: the existence of a risk-free asset, multivariate stable distribution with common exponent for random returns, and a convex, positively homogeneous dispersion measure. Ziemba also considered a special class of dependent multivariate stable distributions.

The problems considered in the previous chapters are static, typically involving the utility of terminal wealth. But actual investment problems are dynamic, with the distributions over asset returns being a stochastic, dynamic process. Brandt and Santa-Clara (2006) consider a dynamic problem with a special perspective. The dynamic portfolio selection problem is approximated by a static portfolio problem defined on an expanded asset space. The static problem on expanded space inherits all the powerful results of static portfolio theory.

The key to the expanded asset space is a set of managed portfolios which are generated by state variables. (There is a rich literature on factors which affect the distributions of returns on risky assets, e.g., Jacobs and Levy (1988), Rosenberg (1974), Rosenberg *et al.* (1985), Fama and French (1992). It is assumed that the investments in basis assets at time t, x_t, are linear in state variables z_t: $x_t = \theta z_t$. The investments in a basis asset x_{it} is split into components associated with each of the state variables, $\tilde{x}_i = (\theta_{i1}, \ldots, \theta_{iK})$, creating an expanded set of assets. The expanded set can be viewed as "managed" portfolios each of which invests in a single basis asset in proportion to the value of a state variable. The returns on the basis assets are split by state variable, $\tilde{R}_{i,t+1} = (R_{i,t+1} \times z_{1t}, \ldots, R_{i,t+1} \times z_{Kt})$. The following quadratic utility problem is solved for the optimal weights in the expanded assets:

$$\max_{\tilde{x}} E\left[\tilde{x}'\tilde{R}_{t+1} - \frac{\gamma}{2}\tilde{x}'\tilde{R}_{t+1}\tilde{R}'_{t+1}\tilde{x}\right].$$

The investments in the basis assets are recovered by adding the component weights. Imbedded in this approach are values of the state variables, but Brandt and Santa-Clara present a statistical model for state variables — VAR, which can be estimated with a modest time series. Although the MV problem is solved for investment decisions, other utilities could be used in a two-step procedure with the expanded assets.

Hanoch and Levy (1969) show that stochastic dominance can be defined by classes of utilities as characterized by higher order derivatives of the utility, so that $U_k = \{u|(-1)^{j-1}u^{(j)} \geq 0, j = 1, \ldots, k\}$, with $u^{(k)}$ being the kth derivative. Then $U_1 \supset U_2 \supset \ldots$. It is standard to define investment decision problems on U_2, the class of non-decreasing, concave utilities. The concave objective is important for optimization, and concavity reflects risk aversion on the part of the decision maker.

There are aspects of risk aversion which are not captured by concavity alone. Pratt (1964) introduces an additional property of utility, decreasing absolute risk aversion (DARA). Arrow (1965) independently discussed decreasing risk aversion in his lectures in Finland. Let $U(x)$ be a utility function for money. The function $\rho(x) = -\frac{u^{(2)}(x)}{u^{(1)}(x)}$ is defined as a measure of local risk aversion or risk aversion in the small, the Arrow–Pratt index. It is shown that a decision maker's local risk aversion $\rho(x)$ is a decreasing function of x ($\rho' < 0$) if and only if, for every risk, his cash equivalent is larger the larger his assets, and his risk premium and what he would be willing to pay for insurance are smaller. This condition, to which many decision makers would subscribe, involves the third derivative of u. Third degree stochastic dominance requires $u^{(3)} \geq 0$ and $\rho' < 0 \implies u^{(3)} > 0$. If U_D is the class of non-decreasing, concave, decreasing absolute risk version utilities, then $U_D \subset U_3$. Vickson (1975, 1977) considered stochastic dominance tests for DARA. Li and Ziemba (1989, 1993) consider optimal portfolio analysis and risk premiums for univariate and multivariate risk aversion.

The class U_D is difficult to characterize. Pratt defines a measure of relative risk aversion $\rho^*(x) = x\rho(x) = -\frac{xu^{(2)}(x)}{u^{(1)}(x)}$, and identifies the class of constant relative risk aversion utilities (CRRA). If U_C denotes the CRRA family of utilities, then $U_C \subset U_D$. Furthermore, the equation $-\frac{xu^{(2)}(x)}{u^{(1)}(x)} = \alpha$ can be solved for the function u, with the solution: $u(x) = \frac{1}{1-\alpha}x^{1-\alpha}, \alpha < 1$. When $\alpha = 1$, the utility is $u(c) = \log(c)$.

The CRRA class of utilities is often used in the analysis of investment decisions. The parameter α captures the aversion to risk, and the impact of risk aversion on investment decisions can be analyzed analytically.

The Arrow–Pratt risk aversion measure is local, that is, it depends on the level of wealth. Rubinstein [1973] developed a measure of global risk aversion in the context of a parameter-preference equilibrium relationship:

$$\Upsilon(x_0) = \frac{-x_0 E\{u^{(2)}(x)\}}{E\{u^{(1)}(x)\}},$$

where x_0 is the initial wealth level and expectation is with respect to the distribution of wealth. (Some properties of this measure in the context of risk aversion with changing initial wealth levels appear in Kallberg and Ziemba (1983).) This measure is less tractable and less familiar than the Arrow–Pratt measure. In contrast to the Arrow–Pratt measure which is a function of wealth x, Υ is a constant. Except for a few special cases, Υ does not have a simple form. For quadratic utility, $\Upsilon(1) = \rho(\bar{x})$; thus the Rubinstein measure is the Arrow–Pratt measure evaluated at the expected final wealth level.

For the optimal investment problem, Kallberg and Ziemba establish an important property of the global risk measure. The investor's problem is

$$\max Eu(R'x), s.t. e'x = 1, x \in K.$$

where E represents expectation with respect to the randomness in $R' = (R_1, \ldots, R_n)$, the vector of risky asset returns. K is a convex set that represents additional constraints on the choice of x.

> *Optimality of Rubinstein's Risk Aversion Measure.*
> Investors with the same Υ have the same optimal portfolios regardless of their wealth and utility functions.

They also show with empirical studies that investors with similar average Arrow–Pratt risk aversion have similar portfolios, regardless of their utility function. The results also yield the following conclusions:

- The special exponential and negative power utility functions yield very risk averse portfolios, while the positive power utility function yields highly risky portfolios and moderately risk averse portfolios for different values of α.
- The arctangent utility function usually yields highly risky portfolios.
- The quadratic, exponential and logarithmic utility functions yield the largest range in variation of ρ and yield the safest and riskiest portfolios.
- The quadratic utility function may well play a useful role as a computational surrogate for more plausible utility functions when the number of possible investment securities is large, say $n > 50$.
- With horizons of a year or less one can substitute easily derived surrogate utility functions that are mathematically convenient for more plausible but mathematically more complicated utility functions and feel confident that the errors produced in the calculation of the optimal portfolios are at most of the order of magnitude of the errors in the data.
- Calculations indicate that the maximum expected utility and optimal portfolio composition are relatively insensitive to errors in estimation of the variance–covariance matrix. However, errors

in estimating the mean return vector do significantly change these quantities.

Chopra and Ziemba (1993), following the earlier papers of Kallberg and Ziemba (1981, 1984), consider the relative impact of estimation errors and the impact of risk aversion on portfolio performance. Mean percentage cash equivalent loss due to errors in means, variances and covariances in a mean-variance model are found to be in relative terms roughly 20:2:1 times as important, respectively.

The error depends on the risk tolerance, the reciprocal of the Arrow–Pratt risk aversion $\rho(x)$.

With low risk aversion, like log utility the ratios can be 100:2:1. So good estimates of asset return distribution moments are the most crucial aspect for successful application of a mean-variance analysis, and in all other stochastic modeling approaches. The sensitivity of the mean carries into multiperiod models. There the effect is strongest in period 1, then less and less in future periods, see Geyer and Ziemba (2008).

The impact of modeling and estimation errors on forecasts for securities prices and the resulting effect on portfolio decisions and capital accumulation have been considered in other studies. Pastor and Stambaugh (1999) conclude that model error is less important than estimation error; see also Kallberg and Ziemba (1981) who conclude the same. With regard to estimation error, alternative estimates for the mean return have been considered in a long series of asset prices (Grauer and Hakansson, 1995), with improved results from shrinkage (Stein) estimators. MacKinlay and Pastor (2000) use a restriction, which incorporates the covariance of returns to calculate an estimate of expected returns which is superior to the shrinkage estimator.

MacLean, Foster and Ziemba (2007) use a Bayesian framework to include the covariance in an estimate of the mean. In essence, the return on one asset provides information about the return on related assets, and the sharing of information through the covariance improves the quality of estimates (Jones and Shanken, 2003).

The significance of quality estimates for model parameters is highlighted when those values become inputs to portfolio decisions and the accumulation of wealth over time. This process is illustrated for the portfolio selection problem with constant relative risk aversion utility. That utility enables a closed form solution which depends on the conditional expected return. With the CRRA utility, the loss in wealth resulting from estimation errors can be mitigated with the risk aversion parameter. In the decision rule, the risk aversion parameter α defines a fraction $\frac{1}{1-\alpha}$ of capital invested in the optimal portfolio. When $\alpha < 0$, the control of decision risk also reduces the impact of estimation error. Correspondingly, when $\alpha > 0$, the overinvestment increases the effect of estimation error.

Expected utility theory certainly captures some of the intuition for risk aversion over very large stakes. But the theory is manifestly not close to the right-explanation for most risk attitudes, and does not explain the modest-scale risk aversion observed in practice. Rabin and Thaler (2001) think that the correct explanation incorporates two concepts: loss aversion and mental accounting.

Loss aversion is the tendency to feel the pain of a loss more acutely than the pleasure of an equal-sized gain. Loss aversion is incorporated in Tversky's Kahneman and prospect theory (1979), which models decision makers who react to changes in wealth, rather than levels, and are roughly twice as sensitive to perceived losses than to gains.

Mental accounting, which refers to the tendency to assess risks in isolation rather than in a broader overall perspective. If investors focus on the long-term returns of stocks they would recognize how little risk there is, relative to bonds, and would be happy to hold stocks at a smaller equity premium. Instead, they consider short-term volatility, with frequent mental accounting losses, and demand a substantial equity premium as compensation.

Rabin and Thaler (2001) argue that loss aversion and the tendency to isolate each risky choice must both be key components of a good descriptive theory of risk attitudes.

A possible explanation for the forward premium puzzle is provided by behavioral finance. It is proposed that there are heuristic biases in decision making (Fuller, 1998). Kahneman and Tversky (1979) identify a "representativeness bias", where investors overweigh recent patterns in returns. Another important bias follows from "overconfidence", where investors overestimate the accuracy of their forecasts (Burnside *et al.* (2010)).

The overreaction to information results in overshooting in the forward exchange rate and spot rate, with the error greater in the forward rate. This produces a forward premium, but the overreaction in the spot rate is subsequently reversed. The forward premium bias is greater when investors are more overconfident and this is seen in high trading volume and excess volatility.

The models with market regimes and behavioral bias cannot be together in the theory for interest rate parity. Often investor expectations are unbiased, but under certain conditions there are decision biases. Periods with high volatility and large spreads have negative premiums following from overconfidence and conversely low volatility and tight spreads are associated with positive premiums. The periods with common characteristics and biases are called regimes.

MacLean *et al.* (2012) show that the covered interest rate parity does not hold in its usual sense but does hold in a weak version. There are regimes over time and that the risk premiums on the hedged currency investments are constant across all currencies within each regime but differ across regimes.

Readings

Arrow, K. (1965). The theory of risk aversion, in *Aspects of the Theory of Risk Bearing*, Y. J. Saatio, (ed.) Reprinted in *Essays in the Theory of Risk Bearing*. Chicago: Markham Publ. Co. 1971, 90–109.

Burnside, C., Han, B., Hirshleifer, D. and Wang, T. (2010). Investor overconfidence and the forward premium puzzle, *Review of Economic Studies*, **78**: 523–558.

Brandt, M. and Santa-Clara, P. (2006). Dynamic portfolio selection by augmenting the asset space, *Journal of Finance* **61**: 2187–2217.

Chopra, V. and Ziemba, W. T. (1993). The effect of errors in mean and co-variance estimates on optimal portfolio choice, *Journal of Portfolio Management*, (Winter): 6–11.

Fama, E. F. and French, F. (1992). The cross-section of expected stock returns, *Journal of Finance*, **47** June: 427–466.

Fuller, R. J. (1998). Behavioral finance and the sources of alpha, *Journal of Pension Plan Investing*, **2**: 2–21.

Geyer, A. and Ziemba, W. T. (2008). The innovest Austrian pension fund financial planning model innoALM, *Operations Research* **56**: 797–810.

Grauer, R. R., and Hakansson, N. H. (1995). Stein and CAPM estimators of the means in asset allocation, *International Review of Financial Analysis* **4**: 721–739.

Hanoch, G. and Levy, H. (1969). The efficiency analysis of choices involving risk, *Review of Economic Studies*, **36**(3): 335–346.

Jacobs, Bruce I. and Levy, K. N. (1988). Disentangling Equity Return Regularities: New Insights and Investment Opportunities. *Financial Analysts Journal*, May/June 1988.

Jones, C. S. and Shanken, J. (2003). Mutual fund performance with learning across funds, *Journal of Financial Economics* **78**(3): 507–552.

Kahneman, D. and Tversky, A. (1979). Prospect theory: An analysis of decisions under risk, *Econometrica* **47**(2): 263–291.

Kallberg, J. G. and Ziemba, W. T. (1981). Remarks on Optimal Portfolio Selection, in *Methods of Operations Research*, G. Bamberg and O. Opitz (eds.). Cambridge, MA: Oelgeschlager, Gunn and Hain, Ch 44, 507–520.

Kallberg, J. G. and Ziemba, W. T. (1983). Comparison of alternative utility functions in portfolio selection problems, *Management Science* **XXIX**: 1257–1276.

Kallberg, J. G. and Ziemba, W. T. (1984). Mis-specifications in portfolio selection problems, in *Risk and Capital, Lecture Notes in Economics and Mathematical Systems*, G. Bamberg and K. Spreemann (eds.). Berlin: Springer, Vol. 227, 74–87.

Kelly, J. R. (1956). A new interpretation of the information rate, *Bell System Technical Journal*, **35**: 917–926.

Li, Y. and Ziemba, W. T. (1989). Characterizations of optimal portfolios by univariate and multivariate risk aversion, *Management Science* **35**: 259–269.

Li, Y. and Ziemba, W. T. (1993). Univariate and multivariate measures of risk aversion and risk premiums, *Annals of Operations Reserch* **45**: 265–296.

MacKinlay, A. C. and Pastor, L. (2000). Asset pricing models: Implications for expected returns and portfolio selection, *The Review of Financial Studies* **13**(4): 883–916.

MacLean, L. C., Foster, M. and Ziemba, W. T. (2007). Covariance complexity and rates of return on assets, *Journal of Banking and Finance* **31**(11): 3503–3523.

MacLean, L. C., Zhao, Y. and Ziemba, W. T. (2012). Currency returns, market regimes and behavioral biases, *Annals of Finance* **9**(2): 249–269.

Markowitz, H. M. (1952). Portfolio selection, *Journal of Finance* **7**: 77–91.

Markowitz, H. M. (1959). *Portfolio Selection: Efficient Diversification of Investments.* New York: Wiley and Sons.

Markowitz, H. M. (1987). *Mean-Variance Analysis in Portfolio Choice and Capital Markets.* Cambridge, MA: Basil Blackwell.

Markowitz, H. M. and Van Dijk, E. (2006). Risk-return analysis in *Handbook of Asset and Liability Analysis*, Vol. 1, S. A. Zenios and W. T. Ziemba (eds.), Amsterdam: Elsevier, 139–197.

Pastor, L., Stambaugh, R.F. (1999). Costs of equity capital and model mispricing, *Journal of Finance* **54**: 67–121.

Pratt, J. W. (1964). Risk aversion in the small and in the large, *Econometrica* **32**: 122–136.

Rabin, M. and Thaler, R. A. (2001). Anomalies: Risk aversion, *Journal of Economic Perspectives* **15**(1): 219–232.

Rosenberg, B. (1974). Extra market components of covariance in securities markets, *Journal of Financial and Quantitative Analysis* **9**(2): 263–274.

Rosenberg, B., Reid, K. and Lanstein, R. (1985). Persuasive evidence of market inefficiency, *Journal of Portfolio Management* **11**(3): 9–16.

Rubinstein, M. E. (1973). The fundamental theorem of parameter difference security valuation, *J. of Financial and Quantitative Analysis*, 8, 61–70.

Tobin, J. (1958). Liquidity preference as behavior towards risk, *Review of Economic Studies* **25**: 65–86.

Vickson, R. G. (1975). Stochastic dominance for decreasing absolute risk aversion, *Journal of Financial and Quantitative Analysis* **10**(5): 799–811.

Vickson, R. G. (1977). Stochastic orderings from partially known utility functions, *Mathematics of Operations Research* **2**(3): 244–252.

Ziemba, W. T., Parkan, C. and Brooks-Hill, F. J. (1974). Calculation of investment portfolios with risk free borrowing and lending, *Management Science* **XXI**(2): 209–222.

Ziemba, W. T. (1975). Choosing investment portfolios when the returns have stable distributions, in *Stochastic Optimization Models in Finance*, W. T. Ziemba and R. G. Vickson (eds.), Waltham Academic Press. Reprinted from *Mathematical Programming: Theory and Practice*. Amsterdam: North Holland (1974), 443–482.

Appendix D: Optimization

Estimation of Returns

Consider $\{P_{1t}, \ldots, P_{Kt}\}$, the prices of K risky securities at time $t, t = 1, \ldots, T$. Then $Y_{it} = \ln(\frac{P_{it}}{P_{i,t-1}})$ is the rate of return in period $t, t = 1, \ldots, T$. The distribution of $Y_t' = (Y_{1t}, \ldots, Y_{Kt})'$, $t = 1, \ldots, T$ is the basis of investment decisions. Assuming that Y_t is multivariate normal and stationary, the relevant parameters in the distribution are $E(Y_t) = \mu = (\mu_1, \ldots, \mu_K)'$, $\mathrm{var}(Y_t) = \Sigma = (\sigma_{ij})$.

Given observations $y_t' = (y_{1t}, \ldots, y_{Kt})'$, $t = 1, \ldots, T$, the sample mean $\bar{y}$ and sample covariance S are the traditional estimates for μ and Σ, respectively. There are modifications to the usual maximum likelihood estimates which reduce estimation error. For the estimation of mean return some adjusted estimators are:

1. Stein: mean reversion — shrinking sample means towards a global mean $\bar{\bar{y}}$

$$\hat{\mu}_{Stein} = \bar{\bar{y}}1 + \left(\frac{n}{\varphi + K}\right)(\bar{y} - \bar{\bar{y}}1)$$

$$\varphi = \frac{K + 2}{(\bar{y} - \bar{\bar{y}}1)'S^{-1}(\bar{y} - \bar{\bar{y}}1)}.$$

2. Covariance: common information — adjustment towards an equilibrium value μ_e

$$\hat{\mu}_{Bayes} = \mu_e + (I - DS^{-1})(\bar{y} - \mu_e), \quad D = diag(S - LL'),$$

where L = matrix of subset of eigenvectors.

Portfolio

For the investment opportunity set of assets with rates of return per period $Y_t' = (Y_{1t}, \ldots, Y_{Kt})'$, $t = 1, \ldots, T$, and investment capital W_{t-1} in period t, the allocation of capital to assets is $(x_{1t}W_{t-1}, \ldots, x_{Kt}W_{t-1})$. So x_{it} is the fraction invested in asset $i, i = 1, \ldots, K$ and $x_{0t} = 1 - \sum_{i=1}^{K} x_{it}$ is the fraction in a riskless asset (or not invested). The portfolio is the investment allocation

$$X = \{X_t, t = 1, \ldots, T\} = \{(x_{1t}, \ldots, x_{Kt})', t = 1, \ldots, T\}.$$

The portfolio decision can be made at the beginning of the planning horizon and be fixed throughout. In that case the portfolio is static. A popular static portfolio is fixed fraction, so that the same fractions hold at each time: $X_t' = (x_{1t}, \ldots, x_{Kt}) = X' = (x_1, \ldots, x_K)$ $gt = 1, \ldots, T$.

Portfolio return

The wealth (accumulated returns) at the end of the horizon is

$$W_T(X) = W_0 \prod_{t=1}^{T} (1 + X_t' Y_t).$$

Let the (mean, covariance) of terminal wealth be

$$(\mu(W_T(X)), \Sigma(W_T(X))).$$

Optimal decision making models

The canonical optimal portfolio problem is

$$\max_x \{E[U(W_T(X))] | X feasible\}.$$

There are variations on this problem depending on the utility U and the conditions for feasibility. In the basic case feasibility is determined by the budget constraint $\sum_{i=0}^{K} x_i = 1$. Therefore short-selling ($x_i < 0$) is feasible, and in particular unlimited borrowing ($x_0 < 0$) at some risk free rate r is permitted. Alternatively it may be required that $x_i \geq 0$, or have bounds $-a \leq x_i \leq b$.

Some classic problems follow from the choice of utility function.

1. Mean-variance: The quadratic utility

$$\max_{X} E[U(W_T(X))] = \max_{X} \left[\mu(W_T(X)) - \frac{\lambda}{2} \Sigma(W_T(X)) \right].$$

An equivalent formulation is

$$\max_{X} \{ \mu(W_T(X)) | \Sigma(W_T(X)) \leq c, X \text{feasible} \}.$$

2. Kelly: Log utility

$$\max_{X} E[U(W_T(X))] = \max_{X} E ln(W_T(X)).$$

3. Fractional Kelly: CRRA

$$\max_{X} E[U(W_T(X))] = \max_{X} E \left[\frac{1}{1 - \gamma} (W_T(X))^{1-\gamma} \right].$$

General optimization problem

Suppose $\mathcal{X} \subset \mathbb{R}^n$ is open, and $f: \mathcal{X} \longrightarrow \mathbb{R}, g: X \longrightarrow \mathbb{R}^m$, and $h: X \longrightarrow \mathbb{R}^k$ are each continuously differentiable. The general constrained maximization problem (CMP) is

$$\max_{x \in X} f(x)$$
$$\text{Subject to } g(x) \geq 0$$
$$h(x) = 0.$$

A vector $x \in \mathcal{X}$ that satisfies the two constraints is called a feasible point. A feasible point x satisfies the Constraint Qualification (CQ) if

(i) rank $h_x(x) = k$, and (ii) there is a $w \in$
$\mathbb{R}^n$ such that $h_x(x)w = 0$; $g^j(x) = 0 \Rightarrow g_x^j(x)w > 0$,

where h_x is the gradient of first derivatives with respect to x.

Lagrangian: $\mathcal{L}$: $\mathbb{R}^n \times \mathbb{R}^m \times \mathbb{R}^k \to \mathbb{R}$ where

$$\mathcal{L}(x, \lambda, \mu) = f(x) + \lambda \cdot g(x) + \mu \cdot h(x).$$

Kuhn–Tucker Conditions

$$\mathcal{L}_x(x, \lambda, \mu) = x + \lambda \cdot g_x(x) + \mu \cdot h_x(x) = 0$$
$$\mathcal{L}_\lambda(x, \lambda, \mu) = g(x) \geq 0, \quad \lambda \geq 0$$
$$\mathcal{L}_\lambda(x, \lambda, \mu) \cdot \lambda = g(x) \cdot \lambda = 0$$
$$\mathcal{L}_\mu(x, \lambda, \mu) = h(x) = 0.$$

Optimality

- If x^* is optimal for CMP and the CQ is satisfied then there exists (λ^*, μ^*) such that (x^*, λ^*, μ^*) satisfies the Kuhn–Tucker conditions.

- If f is concave, g^j is quasi-concave, and h is affine, and (x^*, λ^*, μ^*) satisfies the Kuhn–Tucker conditions, then x^* is optimal for CMP.

Section D Exercises

[D1] Consider a risk-averse investor with initial wealth w_0 who may invest any portion of w_0 in a risk-free asset with zero return and the remainder in a risky asset with rate of return R, a random variable. Let x be the amount invested in the risky asset and $w_0 - x$ the amount invested in the risk-free asset. The individual chooses x to maximize the expected utility of terminal wealth w, where $w = w_0 + xR$. Let $W(x) = Eu(w_0 + xR)$

(a) Show that

$$W'(x) = E(u'(x)R) \text{ and } W''(x) = E[u''(x)R^2] < 0.$$

(b) Show that $W(x)$ has its maximum at $x = 0$ if and only if $W'(0) \leq 0$. Show that a necessary and sufficient condition for this to occur is that $ER \leq 0$.

(c) Show that $x > 0$ if and only if $ER > 0$. This demonstrates that a risk-averter will always take some part of an actuarially favorable gamble.

Consider the case in which $W(x)$ is maximized at an interior point $x^* \neq 0$. It is of interest to study the behavior of x^* as a function of initial wealth w_0.

(d) Show that

$$\frac{dx^*}{dw_0} = -\frac{E[u''(w^*)R]}{E[u''(w^*)R^2]},$$

where $w^* = w_0 + a^* X^* R$.

Suppose that the investor exhibits decreasing absolute risk aversion, i.e., $\rho(w)$ is non-increasing in w.

(e) Show that $u''(w_0 + x^* R)R \geq -\rho(w_0)u'(w_0 + x^* R)R$.

(f) Show that $E[u''(w_0 + x^* R)R] \geq 0$. This demonstrates that $dx^*/dw_0 \geq 0$, so that the amount of risky investment does not decrease with increasing initial wealth.

(g) Show that $dx^* dw_0 < 0$ if $\rho(w)$ is strictly increasing.

[D2] An investor with utility function $u(w) = -e^{-kw}$ and initial wealth w_0 can invest in a risk-free asset with net rate of return $r \geq 0$ and a risky asset with normally distributed net rate of return Y. Let $\mu = E(Y)$, $\sigma^2 = var(Y)$ and $R = w_0[1 + xY + (1-x)r]$ be terminal wealth given the investment xw_0 in the risky asset.

(a) Show that the investor's preference ordering for the random returns R can be expressed completely in terms of the mean and variance of R.

(b) Show that the investor's mean-variance indifference curves are given by the equations

$$\frac{1}{2} k \sigma_R^2 - \mu_R = l = constant.$$

Show that preference decreases with increasing l.

(c) Show that the optimal investment proportion is

$$x^* = \frac{\pi - r}{k w_0 \sigma^2},$$

if $\mu \geq r$ and borrowing is unlimited.

(d) Suppose the investor is indifferent between a certain return of \$1,000 and a gamble which returns \$0 or \$5,000 with equal probability. Show that $k = 0.657 \times 10^{-3}$.

(e) Suppose that $r = 0.06, \mu = 0.12, \sigma = 0.04, w_0 = \$1,000$. Show that the optimal policy is to borrow \$56,000 and to invest \$57,000 in the risky asset.

What is the optimal policy if $w_0 = \$5,000$?

[D3] For the investor in Exercise [D2] with $w_0 = \$1,000$, initially, find the optimal policy under the following conditions.

(a) Borrowing is limited to \$1,000.

(b) Borrowing is unlimited provided there is at least a 0.99 probability of repaying the loan plus interest.

(c) Borrowing is unlimited provided there is at least a 0.99 probability of repaying the loan, excluding interest.

(d) The loan, excluding interest, must be repaid with probability 1.

[D4] A risky investment returns $(1+y_1) > 1$ with probability $\pi > 0$ and $(1 + y_2) < 1$ with probability $1 - \pi$ Let $\bar{y} = \pi y_1 + (l - \pi) y_2 > 0$ and $\sigma^2 > 0$ be the variance of $\bar{y}$. An investor saves part of his wealth $w_0 > 0$ and invests the balance say x, in the risky investment. Let u be the investor's utility function and suppose that $u' > 0$ and $u'' < 0$.

(a) Show that the optimal investment, say x^* is the solution of $y_1 \pi u'(w_0 + y_1 x) = -y_2(1 - \pi)u'(w_0 + y_2 x)$.

(b) Suppose $u(w) = \ln w$. Show that

$$x^* = -\frac{w_0 \bar{y}}{y_1 y_2} > 0 \quad \text{and} \quad \frac{dx^*}{dw_0} > 0.$$

(c) Suppose $u(w) = w - w^2/2\alpha$, for $\alpha \geq w_0$. Show that

$$x^* = \frac{(\alpha - w_0)\bar{y}}{\sigma^2 + (\bar{y})^2} > 0 \quad \text{and that} \quad \frac{dx^*}{dw_0} < 0.$$

(d) Suppose $u(w) = 1 - e^{-\lambda w}$, for $\lambda > 0$. Show that

$$x^* = \frac{1}{\lambda(y_1 - y_2)} \ln \left(\frac{\pi y_1}{(\pi - 1)y_2} \right) > 0 \quad \text{and that} \quad \frac{dx^*}{dw_0} = 0.$$

(e) Let $\Upsilon(w)$ denote the investor's risk-aversion function. Show that

$$\frac{dx^*}{dw_0} \geq \quad \text{or} \leq 0 \quad \text{if} \ \Upsilon' \geq \quad \text{or} \leq 0.$$

[D5] Show that the model and hence the results in Exercise [D4] apply to the following three investment situations.

(a) A risky investment has initial wealth w_0, saving has a net return r, risky investment has a net return of y_1 wp $\pi > 0$ and y_2 wp $(1 - \pi)$.

(b) An investor has b and L dollars invested in cash and a risky asset. With probability $0 < 1 - \pi < 1$, the risky asset is worthless; otherwise it has value L.

   The investor can insure against loss of any portion z of the risky asset at a cost of pz where $0 < p < 1$.

(c) A foreign exchange speculator owes g English pounds in 90 days. The forward rate of exchange relating dollars to pounds is f. The spot rate of exchange is $s_1 > f$ or $s_2 < f$ with probabilities π and $(1 - \pi)$. Let V be the value of the speculator's other assets in 90 days and h be the amount hedged $0 \leq h \leq g$.

[D6] Consider an investor having a utility function for wealth $u(w)$ which is strictly increasing in w. The risk premium $\pi(w, z)$ for a random return z given initial wealth w_0 is defined by

$$u[w + Ez - \pi(w, z)] = Eu(w + z).$$

Show that if h is any constant

$$\pi(w + h, z) = \pi(w, z + h).$$

[D7] Consider the risk aversion indices

$$\text{Absolute: } \rho(w) = -\frac{u''(w)}{u'(w)};$$

$$\text{Relative: } \varUpsilon(w) = -\frac{wu''(w)}{u'(w)};$$

$$\text{Partial relative: } \Phi(w, h) = -\frac{wu''(w + h)}{u'(w + h)}.$$

(a) Show that $\Psi_\rho(v) = u'[u^{-1}(v)]$ is concave, linear or convex according as $\rho(v)$ is non-decreasing, constant or non-increasing.

(b) Show that $\Psi_\varUpsilon(v) = u^{-1}(v)u'[u^{-1}(v)]$ is concave, linear or convex according as $\varUpsilon(v)$ is non-decreasing constant or non-increasing.

(c) Show that $\Psi_\Phi(v) = u^{-1}(v)u'(u^{-1}(v)) - wu'[u^{-1}(v)]$ is concave, linear or convex according as $\rho(v)$ is non-decreasing, constant or non-increasing.

[D8] Suppose that z is a random variable with distribution function F defined on an interval $[a, b]$. We are interested in the behavior of the risk premium $\pi(w, z)$ as z and w are subject to scale changes. If z is replaced by λz, λ constant, we restrict

a and λ in such a way that $P[w + \lambda z < 0] = 0$, so that the individual can lose at most his total initial wealth.

(a) Show that $\frac{\partial}{\partial \lambda}[\frac{\pi(w,\lambda z\lambda)}{\lambda}] > 0, = 0, < 0$ according as $\Phi(v)$ is non-decreasing, constant or non-increasing.

(b) Let $v = u(w + \lambda z)$. Show that $\frac{\partial}{\partial \lambda}[\frac{\pi(w,\lambda z\lambda)}{\lambda}] > 0, = 0, < 0$ according as $\Upsilon(v)$ is non-decreasing, constant or non-increasing.

(c) Let $v = u(w + \lambda z)$. Show that $\frac{\partial}{\partial w}[\pi(w, z)] > 0, = 0, < 0$ according as $\rho(v)$ is non-decreasing, constant or non-increasing.

(d) Discuss the economic interpretation of the results, particularly regarding local versus global measures of risk aversion.

[D9] Consider the partial relative risk-aversion function $\Phi(w, h)$ and relative risk-aversion function $\Upsilon(w)$.

(a) Let h be fixed. Show that if $\Phi(w, h)$ is non-increasing in w in some interval $(0, w_0)w_0 > 0$, then either $\Phi(w, h) = 0$ or $h = 0$.

(b) Let $h > 0, w_0 > 0$. Show that if $\Phi(w, h)$ is monotone in w then it is non-decreasing for $0 < w, w_0$.

(c) Show that if $\Upsilon(w)$ is non-decreasing, then either $u''(w) = 0$ or $\Phi(w, h)$ is strictly increasing in w for each h.

[D10] A portfolio is efficient if for its expected rate of return, no portfolio exists with a lower variance. Suppose that an investor must allocate his wealth among two risky assets and a riskless assert having zero net return. The two risky assets have mean returns μ_1 and μ_2 and covariance matrix

$$\Sigma = \begin{pmatrix} \sigma_{11}^2 & \sigma_{12} \\ \sigma_{12} & \sigma_{22}^2 \end{pmatrix}.$$

The investment allocations satisfy $-1 \le x_i \le 2, 0 \le \sum x_i \le 1$.

(a) Suppose $\sum = \begin{pmatrix} 0.0004 & 0.0006 \\ 0.0006 & 0.0009 \end{pmatrix}$ and $(\mu_1, \mu_2) = (0.05, 0.10)$. So there is perfect correlation between assets.

Show that the efficient surface is described as follows:

A portfolio $(\frac{1}{3}, -1, \frac{2}{3})$, which has zero variance and expected return 0.0167.

The next points are described by reducing cash to zero and purchasing asset 2 until the portfolio is $(0, -1, 1)$, which has an expected return of 0.5 and standard deviation of 0.1.

The next section of the frontier moves to (0, 0, 1) if the rate of interest on margin loans is exactly equal to $r > 0.05$ or if not, to $(-1, 0, 2)$. If $0.5 < r < 0.10$, the frontier passes from (0, 0, 1) to $(-1, 0, 2)$ and is linear between these points. If $r \geq 0.10$, the efficient surface terminates at (0, 0, 1). Plot this efficient surface, and also the efficient surface corresponding to the constraints $\sum x_i = 1$, $x_i \geq 0$.

Compare these plots paying particular attention to the number of admissible efficient portfolios.

(b) Suppose there is zero correlation, i.e., $\sigma_{12} = 0$. Show that no portfolio with zero variance and positive expected returns exists. Show that the minimum variance portfolio is $\frac{x_1}{x_2} = \frac{\sigma_{11}}{\sigma_{22}}$ if cash is excluded. Recall that this result also holds when short sales and margin loans are not allowed. When should short sales be made?

(c) Consider the case in (b) with $\sigma_{12} = 0$ and other parameters general. Suppose $r \geq x_1^* \mu_1 + (1 - x_1^*) \mu_2$, where $(x_1, 1 - x_1)$ is the minimum risk portfolio. Show that the investor will never acquire a margin loan.

(d) Investigate the case with perfect negative correlation.

[D11] Consider an investor who wishes to allocate B dollars-among n investments. Suppose the return per dollar invested in i is R_i. Let $R = (R_1, \ldots, R_n)'$ and let the mean and variance–covariance matrix of R be μ and Σ, respectively. One way to compute the frontier of the mean-variance efficient surface is to max $\{\mu'x|x'\Sigma x \leq \alpha, e'x = B, x_i \geq 0, i = 1, \ldots, s, s, \leq n\} \equiv \varphi(\alpha)$, for $\alpha \geq 0$.

(a) Prove that $\varphi(\alpha)$ is a concave function of α.

(b) Show hat $\varphi(\alpha)$ is still concave if the constraint $(x'\Sigma x)^{\frac{1}{2}} \leq \alpha$ replaces the constraint $x'\Sigma x \leq \alpha$.

(c) Illustrate the graphical and economic interpretation of (a) and (b).

(d) Show that the optimal x_i/x_j ratios are independent of B. [Hint: Utilize the Kuhn–Tucker conditions.]

(e) Utilize (d) to show that x is on the efficient surface if and only if $x(C/B)$ is on the efficient surface if the investor's initial wealth is C dollars. Hence one may compute the efficient surface utilizing $B = 1$ and then scale the resulting optimal x, so that they sum to B.

   An alternative way to generate the efficient surface is to $\min\{x'\Sigma x|\mu'x \geq \beta, e'x = 1, x_i \geq 0, i = 1, \ldots, s, s \leq n\} \equiv \psi(\beta)$ for all β.

(f) Prove that $\psi(\beta)$ is convex in β.

(g) When can the computations be limited to $\beta \geq 0$.

(h) Assume that the inequality constraints $x'\Sigma x \leq \alpha$ and $\mu'x \geq \beta$ are binding for all α and β. Show that the two approaches give the same efficient surface.

[D12] Referring to Exercise [D11], suppose $s = 0$, i.e., short sales are allowed in all securities. Consider the second formulation

$$f(\beta) = \min\{x'\Sigma x|\mu'x \geq \beta, e'x = 1\}.$$

(a) When is the constraint $\mu'x \geq \beta$ binding?

(b) Assuming that the constraint in (a) is binding show that an equivalent problem is

$$\min\{x'\Sigma x - \lambda(\mu'x - \beta)|, e'x = 1\} \text{ for } \lambda \geq 0.$$

(c) Develop the Kuhn–Tucker conditions and show that the optimal x are linear functions of λ.

(d) Assuming that one wished to compute an efficient frontier, show how the result in (a) might simplify this calculation.

(e) Suppose that Σ is positive definite and μ, β and n, are such that $\mu'x \geq \beta$ is always binding.

Show that the optimal strategy has the form

$$x^* = a_1 + a_2\beta,$$

the optimal value has the form

$$f(\beta) = b_1 + b_2\beta + b_3\beta^2.$$

[D13] If R is a random variable with mean μ and variance σ^2, establish

(a) $P[|R - \mu| \geq \mu - d] \leq \frac{\sigma^2}{(\mu-d)^2}$. Tchebychev's inequality

(b) $P[R \leq d] \leq \frac{\sigma^2}{(\mu-d)^2}$.

Suppose $R = w_0[1 + r + x(Y - r)]$ where $r \geq 0$ and $\geq Y$ is a random variable. Let A^* be the solution set of the problem $\min\{P[R \leq d|x \in A\}$ and A^{**} be the solution set of the problem $\min\left\{\frac{\sigma^2}{(\mu-d)^2}|x \in A\right\}$. Show that $A^{**} \subset A^* A^{**} = A^*$.

(c) Show that $A^{**} \subset A^*$ and interpret this result. When does $A^{**} = A^*$?

What is the corresponding result if x is not restricted to the set A?

[D14] Let $Y_1, \ldots, Y_n$ be multivariate normally distributed with means $\mu_1, \ldots, \mu_n$ and covariance Σ. Let

$$R = w_0\left(1 + x_0 r + \sum_{i=1}^{n} x_i Y_i\right) \quad \text{and} \quad E(R) = \mu_R,$$

with risk free return $(1 + r)$ and investment fractions $(x_1, \ldots, x_n)$.

(a) Show

$$\min \left\{ \Pr[R \le d] \,\middle|\, \sum_{i=0}^{n} x_i = 1, x_0 \ge 0, \mu_R \ge d \right\}$$

is equivalent to

$$\min \left\{ \sigma_R^2/(\mu_R - d)^2 \,\middle|\, \sum_{i=0}^{n} x_i = 1, x_0 \ge 0, \mu_R \ge d \right\}.$$

(b) Show that any solution x^* to the above problem is mean-variance efficient.

(c) Show that $x_0 = 0$ if $d > w_0(1+r)$, $x_0 = 1$ if $d < w_0(1+r)$, and x_0 is undetermined if $d = w_0(1+r)$.

[D15] Suppose u is the exponential utility function $u(w) = 1 - e^{-aw}$, $a > 0$, and $w = \sum_{i=1}^{n} R_i x_i$, where R_i is the return and x_i is the investment in asset i. Suppose that the random vector $R = (R_1, \ldots, R_n)$ is joint-normally distributed with finite mean μ and covariance matrix Σ. Show that the problem of maximizing the expected utility is equivalent to maximizing the concave quadratic function $\mu'x - \frac{a}{2}x'\Sigma x$.

[D16] In most stochastic optimizing models, the sequencing of the decision and random elements of the problem results in different model formulations, algorithms and economic interpretations. Let the utility of decision choice x and random event $R \in D$, defined on probability space (Ω, B, P) be $u(R, x)$. Then these two models are $v_A = \max\{Eu(R, x)|x \in K\}$ and $v_B = E(\max\{u(R(\omega, x)|x \in K, \omega \in \Omega)\})$, where K is the domain of x.

(a) Show that $v_B \ge v_B$.

(b) Suppose $u(R, x) = f(x) + g(x)R + h(R)$. Show that the optimal decisions for the models are identical.

(c) When is $v_B = v_B$?

(d) Show that optimal decisions under these two approaches are the same if K is the interval $[a, b]$, $u(R, x) =$

$n(R)m(x)$, where n is non-negative and m is monotone non-decreasing on $[a, b]$.

(e) Illustrate other combinations of restrictions on μ, K, D for which optimal decisions are the same.

[D17] Consider a portfolio problem where the only actions available are bets on the occurrence of states of nature. Let R_i be the return per dollar invested in i if state i occurs; investment in i produces no return if j occurs $(i \neq j)$. Assume that the number of states of nature is finite. Let x_i be the amount bet on the occurrence of i out of initial wealth one dollar. Suppose that the investor wishes to maximize expected utility of final wealth, and that the utility function is concave and differentiable.

(a) Suppose that the investor allocates all his resources and p_i is the probability that i occurs. Show that the Kuhn–Tucker conditions are

$$p_i R_i u'(R_i x_i) = \lambda, \quad \text{if } x_i > 0,$$
$$p_i R_i u'(0) \leq \lambda, \quad \text{if } x_i = 0,$$
$$\text{and } \Sigma x_i = 1, \quad x_i \geq 0.$$

(b) Suppose $u(w) = \log(w)$. Show that $x_i^* > 0$ and the objective becomes $\sum p_i \log(x_i) + \sum p_i \log(R_i)$. Show that $x_i^* = p_i$ independently of the returns R_i. Interpret.

(c) Suppose the investor considers holding some of his wealth in reserve so that $\sum x_i \leq 1$. Suppose $u'(0) = \infty$. Show that the individual will invest all his resources if and only if there exists a system of bets such that the individual cannot lose.

(d) Show that the existence of the set of sure bets is sufficient for the investor to invest all his wealth even if $u'(0) < \infty$. Show that this condition is not necessary however, if $u'(0) < \infty$. (Let u be linear, and suppose $p_j R_j > 1$ for some j.)

(e) Show that the optimal bets in (b) are not necessarily sure bets in the sense of (c) even if such a sure bet exists.

[D18] Under certain assumptions, such as quadratic preferences or normally distributed random returns, the mean-variance approach is consistent with the expected utility approach. To provide generality to the risk-return approach it is desirable to be able to consider a risk-return measure that is free of such restrictions on the utility function or the probability distributions. Let $\phi = u(\mu) - E(u(W))$ be a generalized risk measure, where $\mu = E(W)$ is expected wealth and u is the utility function over wealth. Note that unlike the variance, ϕ depends on both u and the distribution of returns; and ϕ makes it possible to represent expected utility in terms of two parameters, (μ, ϕ), without imposing restrictions on the form of u or the distribution of W.

(a) Show that $\phi > 0$ (<0) if u is strictly concave (convex) and zero of u is linear.

(b) The risk premium π is defined by the equation $u(\mu - \pi) = E(u(W))$, so that ϕ is related to π by $\phi = u(\mu) - u(\mu - \pi)$. Suppose that u is strictly increasing; show that $\phi \gtreqless 0$ iff $\pi \gtreqless 0$.

(c) Suppose $u(w)$ is linearly transformed into $v(w) = au(w) + b$. Show that ϕ is transformed to $a\phi$.

(d) Use a Taylor expansion of u about μ to show that $\phi = -\sum_{k=2}^{\infty} \frac{u^{(k)}(\mu)}{k!} M_k$, where M_k, assumed finite, is the kth moment of W about μ.

(e) Suppose W is normally distributed. Show that ϕ is proportional to variance.

(f) Show that ϕ is proportional to variance if utility is quadratic.

[D19] Suppose an investor has the power utility function $u(w) = \frac{1}{\gamma}w^{\gamma}$. Let $R_i > 0$ be the return per dollar invested in i if state i occurs; investment in i produces no return if j occurs

$(i \neq j)$. Assume that the number of states of nature is finite. Let $x_i \geq 0$ be the amount bet on the occurrence of i out of initial wealth of \$1. Suppose the investor wishes to maximize expected utility:

(a) Show that if x^* is an expected utility maximizing alloca- tion, then each x_i^* a decreasing function of R_i if and only if $\gamma < 0$.

(b) Show that if x^* is an expected utility maximizing allo- cation, then each x_i^* an increasing function of R_i if and only if $0 < \gamma < 1$.

[D20] Suppose that X_1 denotes the distribution of returns in period one, and X_2 the distribution of returns in period two. The returns are identical and independent over time (i.i.d.). X_1 and X_2 are given by:

$X_1(= X_2)$	
Outcome	Probability
0.9	1/3
1.2	1/3
1.5	1/3

(a) Draw the one-period cumulative distribution $F(X_1) = F(X_2)$ and calculate the mean and the variance of the random variables.

(b) Draw the two-period distribution $F(X_1 \cdot X_2)$ and calculate the mean and the variance of $X_1 \cdot X_2$.

(c) Is the two-period variance equal to twice the one period variance? Explain.

(d) Suppose that the one-period return is normally distributed. Can a risk averter who invests for two periods choose her investments by the mean-variance rule? Explain.

Exercise Source Notes

Exercise [D1] is adapted from Ziemba–Vickson (1975): p. 174 # 10.
Exercise [D2] is adapted from Ziemba–Vickson: p. 179 # 22. Exercise [D3] is adapted from Ziemba–Vickson: p. 179 # 23. Exercise [D4] is adapted from Ziemba–Vickson: p. 179 # 24. [D5] p. 179 # 25. Exercise [D6] is adapted from Ziemba–Vickson: p. 187 # 8. Exercise [D9] is adapted from Ziemba–Vickson: p. 188 # 9. Exercise [D10] is adapted from Ziemba–Vickson: p. 334 # 11. Exercise [D11] is adapted from Ziemba–Vickson: p. 336 # 13. Exercise [D12] is adapted from Ziemba–Vickson: p. 336 # 14. Exercise [D13] is adapted from Ziemba–Vickson: p. 338 # 20. Exercise [D14] is adapted from Ziemba–Vickson: p. 339 # 21. Exercise [D15] is adapted from Ziemba–Vickson: p. 343 # 1. Exercise [D16] is adapted from Ziemba–Vickson: p. 344 # 4. Exercise [D17] is adapted from Ziemba–Vickson: p. 347 # 12. Exercise [D18] is adapted from Ziemba–Vickson: p. 347 # 17. [D19] is adapted from Ziemba–Vickson: p. 353 # 20.

SECTION E: RISK MEASURES

The concepts of utility and risk attitude such as decreasing risk aversion are general and qualitative. But risk is a basic to decision making models and requires a precise definition. The essential characteristics of risk are the chance of a potential loss and the size of the potential loss. If financial decisions are to be considered in the framework risk management, it is clear that a quantitative measure of risk is needed.

Originally risk was variance. Markowitz (1952) provided a quantitative framework for measuring portfolio risk and return using mean and variance. At the same time, Roy (1952) stated that an investor will prefer safety of principal first and will set some minimum acceptable return that will conserve the principal. This focused on the lower partial moment (LPM).

The returns on investment are uncertain, so that the financial status is given by a random variable X with a distribution function F.

A risk measure is a functional $p(x)$ which depends only on the distribution function F, so that two random variables with the same distribution have the same risk values.

This property is called *law invariance*. Given that risk preferences have been formulated through utility and stochastic dominance, it is reasonable that the ordering of random variables with a risk measure should be consistent with the ordering from stochastic dominance.

The financial position X depends on the uncertain returns on assets and the investment decision, which determines the amount of capital allocated to various assets. It is assumed that the unit returns on assets are functions on a probability space (Ω, B, P), and the set of possible investment strategies determines a class of financial positions χ, with $X \in \chi$. So the risk measure is a functional $\rho \colon \chi \to \mathbb{R}$.

From a financial perspective, it is natural to associate risk as loss of money (Kusy and Ziemba (1986)), and to view the financial risk of X as the capital requirement $\rho(X)$ to make the position X acceptable (Acerbi (2002), Artzner *et al.* (1999), Föllmer and Knispel (2013)). The *acceptance set* of ρ is

$$A_\rho \colon \{X \in \chi | \rho(X) \leq 0\}.$$

The risk measure can be defined from the acceptance set

$$\rho(X) = inf\{m \in \mathbb{R} | X + m \in A_\rho\}.$$

Rockafellar and Ziemba (2000) established the following:

Equivalence Theorem

There is a one-to-one correspondence between acceptance sets A_ρ *and the risk measures* ρ.

The concept of capital requirement to cover the losses from investment captures the financial risk idea, but the probability of loss is not taken into account. A variety of measures, which use the distribution have been proposed and used in risk management practice. Details on the measures are provided in Ogryczak and Ruszczynski (1999) Krokhmal, *et al.* (2011), Föllmer and Knispel (2013) and Föllmer and Schied (2002).

[1] Variance

Markowitz (1952a, 1987) used the variance of the position X to measure risk

$$\rho(X) = E(X - EX)^2,$$

where $E(X)$ is the mean of X. Variability or uncertainty does capture aspects of risk, but the gains are treated the same as losses. Also variance is not consistent with stochastic dominance.

[2] Semi-variance

A better estimate of risk exposure or downside risk was proposed by Markowitz (1959) and Porter (1974) with the semi-variance

$$\rho(X) = E(X - EX)^2_-,$$

where $(.)_-$ denotes negative values.

[3] Deviation Risk Measures

Rockafellar *et al.* (2006) generalized the variance type measure with any square integrable deviation measure: $\chi \longrightarrow \mathbb{R}^+$. Then the risk measure is

$$\rho(X) = D(X) - EX.$$

There is a one-to-one relationship between averse risk measures and deviation risk measures through the relationship $D(X) = \rho(X - EX)$ (see Krokhmal *et al.*, 2011). The aversion property follows from $\rho(X) > \rho(EX)$ for non-constant X.

[4] Value-at-Risk (VaR)

This focus on downside risk measures started with the development of the LPM risk measure by Bawa (1975) and Fishburn (1977). This very popular risk measure was further developed by Rockafellar and Urysasev (2000, 2002) and Jorion (2006). It is defined by the αth quantile of the distribution F for the financial position X

$$\rho(X) = VaR_\alpha(X) = F^{-1}(\alpha) = inf\{x \in \mathbb{R} | F(x) \geq \alpha\}.$$

In terms of losses, VaR_α is the maximum possible loss at the level the confidence level $1 - \alpha$. This measure accounts for losses and probabilities in the sense that it has acceptance sets $A_\rho = \{X \in \chi | VaR_\alpha(X) \leq 0\}$.

VaR is used in governance for endowments, trusts, and pension plans. Worldwide adoption of the Basel II Accord further established this measure as the standard.

[5] AVaR

The VaR measure does not account for the losses below it, as all losses below the cutoff are considered the same. So a variation is to consider the average of the values at risk for $\lambda \in (0, \alpha]$

$$\rho(X) = AVaR_\alpha(X) = \frac{1}{\alpha} \int_0^\alpha VaR_\alpha(X) d\alpha.$$

Föllmer and Knispel (2013) show how AVaR is a building block for law-invariant risk measures.

[6] Conditional Value-at-Risk (CVaR)

A related measure proposed by Rockafellar and Uryasev (2000) and Acerbi and Tasche (2002) and Acerbi (2002) is

$$CVaR_\alpha(X) = E(X|X < F^{-1}(\alpha)).$$

CVaR is the conditional expectation of losses exceeding the $VaR_\alpha(X)$ level. Obviously $CVaR_\alpha(X) = AVaR_\alpha(X)$ when the distribution F for X is continuous. However, for discontinuous distributions, the measures may differ.

As a functional, there exist mathematical properties which may reasonably be expected to be satisfied by risk measures ρ. Those properties can be considered either as properties of the functional or the associated acceptance set.

(A1) Law-invariance: $\rho(X) = \rho(Y)$ for all $X, Y \in \chi$ such that $F_X = F_Y$.

(A2) Monotonicity: $F_X \geq F_Y \Rightarrow \rho(X) \geq \rho(Y)$.

(A3) Translation invariance: $\rho(X + m) = \rho(X) - m$ for all $X \in \chi$, $m \in \mathbb{R}$.

(A4) Sub-additivity: $\rho(X + Y) \leq \rho(X) + \rho(Y)$ for all $X, Y \in \chi$.

(A5) Positive homogeneity: $\rho(\lambda X) = \lambda \rho(X)$ for all $X \in \chi, \lambda > 0$.

(A6) Consistency: $X \ SSD \ Y \Rightarrow \rho(X) \geq \rho(Y)$.

(A7) Risk Aversion: $\rho(X) = c$ for constant c and $\rho(X) > -EX$ for non-constant X.

The properties do not constitute a definition of a risk measure, and they are not sufficient to build a risk measure. For a proposed risk measure, these properties can be verified. Law-invariance is clear. Monotonicity requires that the risk measure is ordered as implied by the distribution, i.e., if one density to the left of the other it implies greater risk. Translation invariance states that adding cash to a financial position reduces the risk by the same amount.

The sub-additivity property is significant since it implies that diversification typically reduces risk, which they usually do. But in a severe crash like what LTCM faced in 1998 with liquidity issues, sub-additivity may not hold. This was part of the motivation for the Rockafellar–Ziemba (2000) axioms. As a set of properties, A2–A5 have been used by Artzner *et al.* (1999) to characterize the class of *coherent risk measures.*

Positive homogeneity and sub-additivity together imply convexity:

$$\rho(\lambda X + (1 - \lambda)Y) \leq \lambda \rho(X) + (1 - \lambda)\rho(Y).$$

Convexity does not imply both positive homogeneity and sub-additivity hold. Since convexity is the desired property, it can replace sub-additivity and homogeneity. The resulting class of convex risk measures is considered in Föllmer and Knispel (2013), following Rockafellar and Ziemba (2000) and Föllmer and Schied (2002). Convexity of the risk measure ρ or the corresponding acceptance set A_ρ is important for decision problems where the risk measure is used to formulate constraints. Averse risk measures, which were introduced by Rockafellar *et al.* (2006) satisfy A4, A5 and A7.

If the commonly used risk measures defined above are checked against the properties, the following results hold:

- Standard deviation: satisfies A1, A5 and A4 if $cov(X, Y) \geq 0$.
- VaR: satisfies A1, A2 and A3.
- AVaR: satisfies A1, A2, A3, A4, A5, A6 and A7.

So AVaR (or CVaR in the case of continuous distributions) has all the properties of a reasonable risk measure.

A general framework for defining a risk measure ρ based on the distribution function F for a financial position X is with a Choquet integral. A distortion function g is defined such that $g: [0, 1] \to [0, 1]$, $g(0) = 0, g(1) = 1$, and g non-decreasing.

Then risk measures are of the form

$$\rho_g(X) = \int\limits_0^\infty g(1 - F(t))dt + \int\limits_{-\infty}^0 [g(1 - F(t)) - 1]dt.$$

The elegance of this formulation is the association of the risk measure with the distortion/weighting of the probability distribution F to capture risk perception. There is a family of risk measures defined by the distortion functionals. Föllmer and Knispel (2013) discuss various such risk measures. The risk measure is convex if and only if the distortion functional is concave. The distortion functional for VaR is not concave, so it is not convex nor consistent with second order stochastic dominance.

The distortion functional operates on the distribution function F, or alternatively on the fixed measure P probability space (Ω, B, P). There are shortcomings of the distortional function approach. In particular, the excessive reliance on a single probabilistic model P. More generally, it raises the issue of model uncertainty or model ambiguity, often called *Knightian uncertainty*. Föllmer and Knispel (2013) discuss a robustification where the probability measure P is a member of a class $\wp$. The class could be the set of probability measures within a specified distance from the reference measure P. On the class the risk measure could be

$$\rho_\wp(X) := \sup_{P \in \wp} \rho_P(X).$$

This set of measures approach could deal with the issue of estimation error. Calculations in MacLean *et al.* (2006) show that the inflation of risk as measured by CVaR can be increased as much as five times from estimation error. That is, an investment strategy chosen to have a CVaR requirement violated 5% of the time, in practice can have a 25% violation. Since the known empirical distribution $\hat{F}$ is an estimate of the true distribution F, the risk measure $\hat{\rho}$ from $\hat{F}$ is an estimate. If F is parametric, then a confidence interval of distributions could define the class over which a risk measure is defined.

In the framework of financial decision making, the management of risk can be viewed in the the style of Markowitz's mean-variance analysis. Krokhmal *et al.* (2011) present the decision problem as a trade-off between risk and reward. Given a payoff (profit) function $X = X(x, \omega)$, that is dependent on the decision vector x and random element $\omega \in \Omega$, the risk measure is $\rho(X) = \rho(X(x, \omega))$ and the reward function is $\pi(X) = \pi(X(x, \omega))$. The problem is to select the decision x that maximizes the reward $\pi(X)$ while assuring that the risk does not exceed ρ_0:

$$\max_{X}\{\pi(X)|\rho(X) \leq \rho_0\}.$$

Alternatively, a weighted combination of risk and reward is optimized:

$$\max_{X}\{\pi(X) - \lambda\rho(X)|\lambda \geq 0\}.$$

In this problem λ is a risk aversion parameter. This penalty parameter may incorporate the potential effects of both model uncertainty and estimation error.

An application with the use of the penalty parameter approach is provided by the financial planning model InnoALM for the Austrian pension fund of the electronics firm Siemens (Geyer and Ziemba, 2008; Ziemba, 2013). The model uses a multi-period stochastic linear programming framework, where uncertainty is modeled using multi-period discrete probability scenarios for random return and other model parameters. The concave risk-averse preference function is to maximize the expected present value of terminal wealth at the specified horizon net of expected discounted convex (piecewise-linear) penalty costs for wealth and benchmark targets in each decision period. Earlier applications of the convex penalty approach are found in Kusy and Ziemba (1986), Ziemba (2003), Cariño and Ziemba (1998) and Cariño *et al.* (1998).

The implementation of a scenario-based asset allocation model leads to more flexible allocation restraints which allows for more risk tolerance and ultimately results in better long-term investment performance.

Readings

Acerbi, C. (2002). Spectral measures of risk: A coherent representation of subjective risk aversion, *Journal of Banking and Finance* **26**: 1505–1518.

Acerbi, C. and Tasche, D. (2002). Expected shortfall: A natural coherent alternative to value-at-risk, *Economic Notes* **31**: 379–388.

Artzner, A. P., Delbaen, F., Eber, J.-M. and Heath, D. (1999). Coherent measures of risk, *Mathematical Finance* **9**(3): 203–228.

Bawa, V. S. (1975). Optimal rules for ordering uncertain prospects, *Journal of Financial Economics* **2**(1): 95–121.

Cariño, D. R. and Ziemba, W. T. (1998). Formulation of the Russell–Yashuda Kasai financial planning model, *Operations Research* **46**: 433–449.

Cariño, D. R., Myers, D. H. and Ziemba, W. T. (1998). Concepts, technical issues, and uses of the Russell–Yashuda Kasai financial planning model, *Operations Research* **46**: 450–462.

Fishburn, P. C. (1977). Mean-risk analysis with risk associated with below-target returns, *American Economic Review* **67**(2): 116–126.

Föllmer, H. and Knispel, T. (2013). Convex risk measures: Basic facts, law-invariance and beyond, asymptotics for large portfolios, in *Handbook of the Fundamentals of Financial Decision Making*, L. C. MacLean and W. T. Ziemba (eds.), Singapore: World Scientific, 507–554.

Föllmer, H. and Schied, A. (2002). Convex measures of risk and trading constraints, *Finance and Stochastics* **6**(4): 429–447.

Geyer, A. and Ziemba, W. T. (2008). The innovest Austrian pension fund planning model InnoALM, *Operations Research* **56**(4): 797–810.

Jorion, P. (2006). *Value at Risk: The New Benchmark for Managing Financial Risk* (3rd edn.). New York: McGraw-Hill.

Krokhmal, P., Zabarankin, M. and Uryasev, S. (2011). Modeling and optimization of risk. *Surveys in Operations Research and Management Science* 16(2): 49–66.

Kusy, M. I. and Ziemba, W. T. (1986). A bank asset and liability management model, *Operations Research* **XXXIV**: 356–376.

MacLean, L., Zhao, Y., and Ziemba, W. T. (2006). Dynamic Portfolio selection with process control. *Journal of Banking and Finance*, **30**(2): 317–339.

Markowitz, H. M. (1952). Portfolio selection, *Journal of Finance* **7**(1): 77–91.

Markowitz, H. M. (1959). *Portfolio Selection: Efficient Diversification of Investments*. New York: Wiley and Sons.

Markowitz, H. M. (1987). *Mean-variance analysis in portfolio choice and capital markets*. Cambridge, MA: Basil Blackwell.

Ogryczak, W. and Ruszczynski, A. (1999). From stochastic dominance to mean-risk models: Semideviation as risk measures, *European Journal of Operations Research* **116**: 33–50.

Porter, R. B. (1974). Semi-variance and stochastic dominance: A comparison, *American Economic Review* **64**(1): 200–204.

Rockafellar, R. T. and Uryasev, S. (2000). Optimization of conditional value-at-risk, *The Journal of Risk* **2**(3): 21–41.

Rockafellar R. T. and Uryasev, S. (2002). Conditional value-at-risk for general loss distributions, *Journal of Banking and Finance* **26**(7): 1443–1471.

Rockafellar, R. T., Uryasev, S. and Zabarankin, M. (2006). Generalized deviations in risk analysis, *Finance and Stochastics* **10**: 51–74.

Rockafellar, R. T. and Ziemba, W. T. (2000). Axiomatic convex risk measures, in *Handbook of the Fundamentals of Financial Decision Making*, L. C. MacLean and W. T. Ziemba (eds.), Singapore: World Scientific.

Roy, A. D. (1952). Safety first and the holding of assets, *Econometrica* **20**(3): 431–449.

Yitzhaki, Shlomo (1982). Stochastic Dominance, Mean Variance, and Gini's Mean Difference, *American Economic Review*, **72**(1): 178–185.

Ziemba, W. T. (2003). *The stochastic programming approach for asset-liability and wealth management*. Virginia: Charlottesville.

Ziemba, W. T. (2013). *The case for convex risk measures, Quantitative Finance Letters*, **1**, 47–54.

Appendix E: Risk Assessment

Risk

Risk is usually defined as a measure of the probability and severity of adverse events. It is the "effect of uncertainty on objectives", where uncertainties include events (which may or may not happen) and uncertainties caused by ambiguity or a lack of information. The key

questions in risk analysis are: What are the possible bad outcomes?
How likely are they? How bad are they? The assessment or appraisal
of adverse events involves preferences and is facilitated by quantitative measures which are consistent with the order implied by preference relations. The measures are key components of risk control
processes. The figure below illustrates the aspects of risk analysis,
appraisal and control.

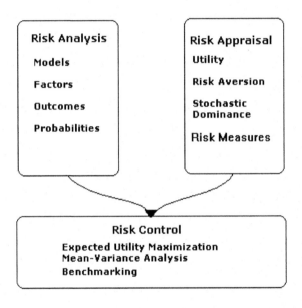

Measures

Theoretically sound and readily evaluated risk measures are the key
to successful risk control. Consider that a performance benchmark is
exogenously established and an adverse event is falling short of the
benchmark. The risk components are (i) the *chances* of a shortfall;
(ii) the *size* of the shortfall. These elements are shown with the probability of the shortfall and the truncated distribution of shortfalls (L)
below.

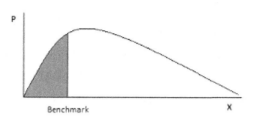

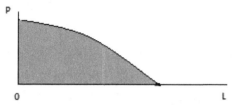

A risk measure ρ is a function mapping the distribution of losses/shortfalls to the real line, that is $\rho\colon (\alpha, L) \to R$. Ideally the measure would incorporate both the chance and size of losses. If the benchmark is arbitrary, it should be considered as a variable, say B, and the conditional risk measure is $\rho(\alpha(B), L(B))$. With a prior distribution/weighting over benchmarks, the marginal risk measure $\bar{\rho}$ could capture the spectrum of risk components.

Properties of measures:
  Monotonicity: $F_X \geq F_Y \Rightarrow \rho(X) \geq \rho(Y)$.
  Sub-additivity: $\rho(X + Y) \leq \rho(X) + \rho(Y)$ for all $X, Y \in \chi$.
  Positive homogeneity: $\rho(\lambda X) = \lambda \rho(X)$ for all.

Bootstrapping

In practice the distribution for outcomes is empirical rather than theoretical and the risk measures are random variables. A standard method of generating a distribution for a sample statistic is bootstrapping. Bootstrapping allows assigning measures of accuracy (defined in terms of bias, variance, confidence intervals, prediction error or some other such measure) to sample estimates. Bootstrapping is the practice of estimating properties of a statistic by measuring those properties when sampling from an approximating distribution. One standard choice for an approximating distribution is the empirical distribution function of the observed data.

The Monte Carlo algorithm for case resampling is quite simple. First, we resample the data with replacement, and the size of the resample must be equal to the size of the original data set. Then the statistic of interest is computed from the resample from the first step. This routine is repeated many times to get a more precise estimate of the bootstrap distribution of the statistic.

There are several methods for constructing confidence intervals from the bootstrap distribution of a theoretical parameter:

- **Basic Bootstrap**. The basic bootstrap is the simplest scheme to construct the confidence interval. Let $\hat{\theta}$ be the sample estimate of θ and θ^* be estimates from bootstrap samples. One simply takes the empirical quantiles from the bootstrap distribution of the parameter:
  $(2\hat{\theta}-\theta^*_{1-\frac{\alpha}{2}}, 2\hat{\theta}-\theta^*_{\frac{\alpha}{2}})$, where $\theta^*_{1-\frac{\alpha}{2}}$ is the denotes the $1-\frac{\alpha}{2}$ percentile of the bootstrapped coefficients θ^*.

- **Percentile Bootstrap**. The percentile bootstrap proceeds in a similar way to the basic bootstrap, using percentiles of the bootstrap distribution, but with a different formula (note the inversion of the left and right quantiles!):
  $(\theta^*_{\frac{\alpha}{2}}, \theta^*_{1-\frac{\alpha}{2}})$, where $\theta^*_{1-\frac{\alpha}{2}}$ denotes $1 - \frac{\alpha}{2}$ percentile of the bootstrapped coefficients θ^*.

This method can be applied to any statistic. It will work well in cases where the bootstrap distribution is symmetrical and centered on the observed statistic and where the sample statistic is median-unbiased and has maximum concentration (or minimum risk with respect to an absolute value loss function). In other cases, the percentile bootstrap can be too narrow. An alternative is the Studentized bootstrap. The Studentized bootstrap works similarly as the usual confidence interval, but uses the quantiles from the bootstrap distribution of the Student's t-test:

- **Studentized Bootstrap.** $\left(\hat{\theta} - t^*_{1-\frac{\alpha}{2}} \times s_\theta, \hat{\theta} - t^*_{\frac{\alpha}{2}} \times s_\theta\right)$, where $t^*_{1-\frac{\alpha}{2}}$ is the $1 - \frac{\alpha}{2}$ percentile of the bootstrapped Student's t-test $t^* = (\hat{\theta}^* - \hat{\theta})/s_{\theta^*}$, where s_θ is the estimated standard error of the coefficient in the original model.

Copulas

A copula is a multivariate probability distribution for which the marginal probability distribution of each variable is uniform. Copulas are used to describe the dependence between random variables. Sklar's Theorem states that any multivariate joint distribution can be written in terms of univariate marginal distribution functions and a copula which describes the dependence structure between the variables.

Copulas are popular in high-dimensional statistical applications as they allow one to easily model and estimate the distribution of random vectors by estimating marginals and copulae separately. There are many parametric copula families available, which usually have parameters that control the strength of dependence. Some popular parametric copula models are outlined below.

Consider a random vector $(X_1, \ldots, X_p)$. Suppose its margins are continuous, i.e., the $F_i(x) = P[X_i \leq x]$ are continuous functions. The random vector $(U_1, \ldots, U_p) = (F_1(X_1), \ldots, F_p(X_p))$ has uniformly distributed marginals. The copula of $(X_1, \ldots, X_p)$ is defined as the distribution function of $(U_1, \ldots, U_p)$:

$$C(u_1, \ldots, u_p) = P[U_1 \leq u_1, \ldots, U_p \leq u_p].$$

The copula C contains all information on the dependence structure between the components of $(X_1, \ldots, X_p)$, whereas the marginal cumulative distribution functions F_i contain all information on the marginal distributions.

The importance of the above is that the reverse of these steps can be used to generate random samples from general classes of multivariate distributions. That is, given a procedure to generate a sample

$(U_1, \ldots, U_p)$ from the copula distribution, the required sample can be constructed as

$$(X_1, \ldots, X_p) = \left(F_1^{-1}(U_1), \ldots, F_p^{-1}(U_p) \right).$$

For illustration consider a given correlation matrix $R \in \mathcal{R}^{p \times p}$. The Gaussian copula with parameter matrix R is

$$C_R^G(u) = \Phi_R \left(\Phi^{-1}(u_1), \ldots, \Phi^{-1}(u_p) \right),$$

where Φ^{-1} is the inverse cumulative distribution function of a standard normal and Φ_R is the joint cumulative distribution function of a multivariate normal distribution with mean vector zero and covariance matrix equal to the correlation matrix R.

Copulas are useful in portfolio/risk management and help us analyze the effects of downside regimes by allowing the modeling of the marginals and dependence structure of a multivariate probability model separately. For example, consider the stock exchange as a market consisting of a large number of traders each operating with his/her own strategies to maximize profits. The individualistic behavior of each trader can be described by modeling the marginals. However, as all traders operate on the same exchange, each trader's actions have an interaction effect with other traders'. This interaction effect can be described by modeling the dependence structure. Therefore, copulas allow us to analyze the interaction effects which are of particular interest during downside regimes as investors tend to herd their trading behavior and decisions.

Section E Exercises

[E1] Consider a random variable X with the set of distributions on $X \colon \mathcal{F}$, and the utility function U. The expected utility with respect to $F \in \mathcal{F}$ is $U(F) = \int u(x) dF(x)$ for some real valued function $u \colon X \to R$. Prove that:

(a) The utility function U has the expected utility form if and only if it is linear in the distribution.

(b) The utility function U has the expected utility form for an affine transformation of u.

[E2] Let X_1 and X_2 be random variables with $E(X_1) \geq E(X_2)$ and $Variance(X_1) \leq Variance(X_2)$. Find a non-decreasing, concave utility u such that $Eu(X_1) < Eu(X_2)$.

[E3] Consider the random variable X, with distribution F_X. Then $\rho(X)$ is a spectral risk measure if $\rho(X) = \int_0^1 \varphi(\alpha) F_X^{-1}(\alpha) d\alpha$, for distortion function φ. Is $VaR_X(\alpha)$ a spectral risk measure?

[E4] Consider the random variable X, with distribution F_X and the utility function u. The certainty equivalent is a number c such that $u(c) = Eu(X)$. The risk premium is the number $\pi = E(X) - c$. Show that a person is risk averse if $\pi > 0$.

[E5] Find $CVaR_X(\alpha)$ for X log-normal $-X \sim LN(\mu, \sigma^2)$.

[E6] Let X be $N(\mu, \sigma^2)$ and check the coherence axioms for $VaR_X(\alpha), \alpha \geq 0.5$.

[E7] Compute the Lorenz curve for $X \sim N(\mu, \sigma^2)$.

[E8] Consider a random sample $X_1, X_2, \ldots, X_n$, on the random variable X with distribution F. If F_n is the empirical distribution determined from the sample, determine $F_n^{-1}(\alpha)$ and compare it to $F^{-1}(\alpha)$. How does $VaR_n(\alpha)$ compare to $VaR(\alpha)$?

[E9] Let X be a random variable with distribution F and $AVaR_X(\alpha)$ be the average value at risk. Show that

(i) $\alpha AVaR_X(\alpha) - (1 - \alpha)AVaR_{-X}(1 - \alpha) = E(X)$.
(ii) $AVaR_X(\alpha) = \max\{y - \frac{1}{\alpha}E([X - y]^-): y \in R\}$.
(iii) $AVaR_X(\alpha) = F^{-1}(\alpha) - \frac{1}{\alpha}E([X - F^{-1}(\alpha)]^-)$.

[E10] Consider random variables X_1 and X_2. Show that $X_1 \ SSD \ X_2$ iff $AVaR_{X_1}(\alpha) \leq AVaR_{X_2}(\alpha)$, for all $\alpha \in (0, 1]$.

[E11] Consider random variables X_1 and X_2. Show that $X_1 \ FSD \ X_2$ iff $VaR_{X_1}(\alpha) \leq VaR_{X_2}(\alpha)$, for all $\alpha \in (0, 1]$.

[E12] Check the coherence axioms for the $AVaR$ and VaR measures.

[E13] The Gini coefficient was introduced as a risk functional by Yitzhaki (1982). If X is a random variable with distribution F, the coefficient is

$$G(X) = \iint |v - u| dF(u) dF(v).$$

Show that

(i) $G(X)$ is positively homogenous.
(ii) The Gini is concave in F.

[E14] Consider the case of a single risky asset w (the market index), with two regimes representing *UP* and *DOWN* markets and a risk-free asset with rate of return r. It is assumed the probabilities for *UP/DOWN* in the coming period are (π_1, π_2). If x units of capital are invested in the conditional risky asset the return in regime $j = 1, 2$ is $R_j(x)$, where

$$R_j(x) = exp\left\{ \left[x(\phi_j - r) + r - \frac{1}{2}x^2\delta_j^2 \right] + x\delta_j Z_j \right\}.$$

Z_j is standard normal. So $\ln(R_j(x)$ is normal with density $f_j(y)$, $j = 1, 2$. The unconditional return $R(x)$ is a mixture of normals with density $f(y) = \pi_1 f_1(y) + \pi_2 f_2(y)$.

If $\bar\phi = \pi_1\phi_1 + \pi_2\phi_2$ and $\bar\sigma^2 = \pi_1\sigma_1^2 + \pi_2\sigma_2^2$, the Kelly strategy invests $x^* = \frac{\bar\phi - r}{\bar\delta^2}$ in the risky asset.

Assume starting wealth is w_0 and the benchmark wealth is w^*. Let $g = \ln(w^*) - \ln(w_0)$. For the Kelly strategy the probability of a shortfall after one period is $\alpha^* = P[R(x^*) < g]$ and the average log-shortfall is $\eta^* = \frac{1}{\alpha^*}\left\{ \int_{-\infty}^{g} [\sum_{i=1}^{2}(g - y)f_i(y)]dy \right\}$.

(a) Express the shortfall rate and average log-shortfall in terms of the parameters $\{(\pi_i, \phi_i, \delta_i), i = 1, 2\}$.

[E15] In the above model, let $r = 0, \phi_2 = (1 - c)\phi_1, \delta_1 = \delta_2$.

(a) Show that the Kelly strategy x^* decreases as c increases.
(b) Show there exists a value g^* such that (i) the shortfall rate and average log-shortfall increase as c increases when

$g > g^*$; (ii) the shortfall rate and average log-shortfall decrease as c increases when $g < g^*$.

[E16] In the two regime model consider parameter values are $\phi_1 = 0.0007, \phi_2 = -0.00126, \delta_1^2 = 0.0001, \delta_2^2 = 0.0008, \pi_1 = 0.75, \pi_2 = 0.25$.

Use these parameter estimates in the computations of shortfall rate and shortfall size for a range of risky investment scenarios. The scenarios are defined by the relative rates in *UP* and *DOWN* regimes, with $= 1 - \frac{\phi_2}{\phi_1}, \phi_1 > 0, \phi_2 < 0$ and the gap $g = \ln(w^*) - \ln(w_0)$. Assume $g < 0$, that is, the wealth at the beginning of the period is above the target. A shortfall occurs if the one period return is less than the gap. Use a middle value of $c = 2.8$.

[E17] Download the 2014 daily return data for the S&P500. Construct the empirical distribution. Find the $\alpha = 0.05$ VaR and the $\alpha = 0.05$ CVaR.

(a) Take 100 bootstrap samples from the empirical distribution and calculate the $\alpha = 0.05$ VaR for each bootstrap sample. Plot the bootstrap distribution for the VaR.

(b) For the bootstrap samples calculate the $\alpha = 0.05$ CVaR for each bootstrap sample. Plot the bootstrap distribution for the CVaR.

(c) Calculate the variance and mean squared error for the bootstrap VaR and CVaR values.

[E18] Multivariate copula

An Archimedian copula has the form: $C(u_1, \ldots, u_p) = \phi^{-1}\{\phi(u_1) + \cdots + \phi(u_p)\}$. The function ϕ is the generator. The Clayton copula has $\phi(u) = \frac{1}{\theta}(u^{-\theta} - 1)$, with $\phi^{-1}(x) = (1 + \theta x)^{\frac{-1}{\theta}}$. Usually $\theta \geq 0$.

Consider two assets with returns

$$X_1 = e^{\mu_1 + \sigma_1 \varepsilon_1} - 1,$$
$$X_2 = e^{\mu_2 + \sigma_2 \varepsilon_2} - 1,$$

where ε_1 and ε_2 are $N(0,1)$. The interdependence between ε_1 and ε_2 is determined by the Clayton copula with parameter θ. High θ gives a strong dependency between assets.

Let $\mu_1 = \mu_2 = 0.005$ and $\sigma_1 = \sigma_2 = 0.005$. Consider an equally weighted portfolio with return $X = 0.5X_1 + 0.5X_2$.

(a) Simulate the standard deviation of the portfolio return for selected values of θ. Plot the standard deviation versus $\frac{1}{\theta}$.

(b) Simulate the 5th percentile of the portfolio return for selected values of θ. Plot the 5th percentile versus $\frac{1}{\theta}$.

SECTION F: DYNAMIC PORTFOLIO THEORY AND ASSET ALLOCATION

The components of financial decision making are financial assets, trading prices, wealth preferences, decision sets, dominance and efficiency. There is a rich literature on financial decision models, where variations on the components are proposed. Some of the models are considered in this final section. Most of the discussion concerns negative power/log utility functions and the associated capital growth. Within the framework of expected utility theory significant qualitative properties of decision behavior can be developed analytically for negative power utility, with log being the most risky power utility function.

An asset class is a group of securities that exhibit similar characteristics, behave similarly in the marketplace, and are subject to the same laws and regulations. The three main asset classes are equities (stocks), fixed income (bonds) and cash equivalents (money market instruments). Additionally, currencies, commodities, real estate and gold are separate asset classes. Asset allocation refers to the specific asset by asset proportional weight in a portfolio.

Strategic asset allocation is passive and describes the practice of creating a portfolio with a mix of assets whose parameters will remain relatively stable over the long term. Because asset prices fluctuate, investors and investment managers may set criteria for rebalancing to the pre-set targets. With a fixed mix, the asset to asset proportions remain constant despite market fluctuation which requires periodic rebalancing.

Tactical asset allocation is active and essentially takes a strategic asset allocation and regularly adjusts it for changing market conditions subject to various forecasts. The premise is that by doing this, one can optimize market exposure to maximize risk-adjusted returns. The primary difference between strategic and tactical asset allocation is active investment management and the belief that it is possible to "beat" the market.

Consider the decision framework, where the investor makes investment decisions constrained by market conditions and capital requirements. The objective is to invest available capital $X(t)$ and consume $C(t)$ in each period, where investment generates wealth, $(X(1), \ldots, X(t-1)) \to W(t)$, through the return on investment, is

$$\max_x E \left\{ \int_0^T U_0(C(t), t) dt + U_1[W(T), T] \right\}.$$

The change in wealth from investment in period t is a geometric process governed by a standard diffusion (random walk) and a jump process. The incremental budget condition is

$$dW = (x'(\alpha - re) + r - C)W dt + W x' \Sigma dZ + \theta_t dN_t(\lambda_t).$$

In addition to investment and consumption decisions being constrained by the available capital, the investor may have financial requirements or goals/targets to meet at the horizon such as:

$$\Pr[W(T) \geq w_{VaR}] \geq 1 - \alpha$$

or

$$\int_{-\infty}^{W_\alpha(T)} w dF_W \geq w_{CVaR}$$

or

$$\Pr[W(T) \geq (1 + \varepsilon)I(T)] \geq 1 - \alpha.$$

Finally, there also may be limits placed on trading which constrain decisions, e.g., short selling and rebalancing.

$$x_{tj} \geq c_t, \quad a_t \leq \frac{x_{tj}}{x_{t-1,j}} \leq b_t.$$

The functions defining the decision model are presented in continuous time, but differencing and summation operators could replace the differential and integral. The richest formulations are discrete time stochastic dynamic models which are solved with multi-period stochastic programming (Ziemba, 2003). The continuous time models yield qualitative results which are useful for characterizing decision behavior.

The utility function is overconsumption at each time period and a bequest function of final wealth. Typically these functions are assumed to be concave risk averse. In the models presented in chapters included in this section, either $U_0 \equiv 0$ or $U_1 \equiv 0$.

The budget constraint defines the change in wealth from the returns on investment and the consumption at each time period. The returns have a diffusive process component $(x'(\alpha - re) + r)W dt$, and a point process (shock) component $\theta_t dN_t(\lambda_t)$. The diffusion is geometric Brownian motion (or a geometric random walk) and the point process is a type of Poisson process. An important feature of the point process is the dependence of the shock intensity on market conditions. This generates clusters of up/down shocks (Consigli *et al.* 2009). Alternatively, the financial market is segmented into scenario regimes (e.g., bull, bear, stable) by shocks. Within a regime the parameters in the price and wealth dynamics are fixed, but differ across regimes. The structure sets up regime dependent decisions (Ma *et al.* 2011).

The goals constraints are variations on the same concept: avoiding downside risk. Market scenarios are defined on a probability space (Ω, B, P), with wealth at the horizon depending on the scenario or trajectory $\omega \in \Omega$. So the probability constraints require that along $(1 - \alpha)$ 100% of trajectories, the final wealth exceeds a level specified either by the fixed value-at-risk, or the value of a trajectory dependent stochastic benchmark portfolio. The integral constraint is a conditional expectation, with the incomplete mean in the αth percentile required to exceed the fixed level w_{CVaR}.

The limits on investment decisions, either on short sales or on the amount of rebalancing, are practical, but they present problems when seeking analytic solutions. However, without the limit conditions investment strategies can be extreme, with highly levered positions and large turnover at rebalancing.

Campbell *et al.* (2003) propose a standard first order autoregressive model for log-returns, with the inclusion of state variables in the dynamics. There are no jump terms that roughly corresponds to the geometric random walk price model in discrete time, but the state variables introduce a time variation in parameters. So the budget equation has the form: $\Delta W_t = (x_t'(\alpha_t - re) + r - C_t)W_t + W_t x_t' \Sigma Z$. (They also consider the case where the short term return r is random.) There are no goal constraints, but the decisions are restricted by $x_{tj} \geq 0$, that is, no short selling or borrowing. The utility in Campbell *et al.* is the Epstein–Zin recursive version

$$U_t = \left\{ (1 - \beta)(C_t)^{\frac{1-\gamma}{\theta}} + \beta E_t[U_{t+1}^{1-\gamma}]^{\frac{1}{\theta}} \right\}^{\frac{\theta}{1-\gamma}}.$$

This is the negative power utility augmented by a conditional expectation over future consumption, where γ is the risk aversion parameter and $\theta = \frac{1-\gamma}{1-\psi^{-1}}$ for an elasticity of intertemporal substitution ψ. This defines the time value of consumption.

Using a log-linearization, the approximate optimal portfolio rule is derived. The rule is the sum of two terms: a myopic component from the vector of excess returns (log optimal solution), and an intertemporal hedging component, which accounts for the fact that asset returns are state dependent and thereby time varying. Without the state dependence the hedging component vanishes.

The myopic rule is usually developed from a decision model which maximizes the utility of wealth at the horizon — the bequest. Barberis (2000) considers this problem with the first order autoregressive model for return dynamics and a negative power utility of terminal wealth

$$U(W(T)) = \frac{1}{1-\gamma}[W(T)]^{1-\gamma}.$$

As in Campbell *et al.*, the state variables generate a time dependence of returns. The decision rule for this problem, when the return parameters and distribution over final wealth specified is known (Merton, 1973). Barberis focuses on the distribution for wealth in the expectation $E(U(W(T))$ when data is available on returns and state variables along the trajectory to the horizon. The return parameters are estimated, either with fixed estimates at the time of decision or with a posterior distribution over parameters. These estimates correspond to assumptions that the parameters are deterministic or random/uncertain, respectively. Barberis analyzes the impact of parameter uncertainty on optimal portfolio decisions. He finds that portfolio calculations can be very misleading if the uncertainty in parameters is ignored. For example, the investor can take positions in stock which are too large and also too sensitive to the predictor variables in the autoregressive model for returns.

The variables affecting the returns on assets have been analyzed in multivariate factor models by Fama and French (1992). These include price to book and small cap variables, see Rosenberg *et al.* (1985). Some of the variables are macroeconomic risk factors such as credit spreads, yield spreads and market indices. Other variables are firm specific financial performance measures such as book-to-market ratios and price earnings ratios. It can be difficult to determine the effects of variables in the multivariate model. Alternatively, the efficiency of a firms operation can be analyzed from financial ratios, and firm efficiency related to market returns. Edirisinghe *et al.* (2013) follow this approach. They consider input dimensions (asset utilization, liquidity, leverage) and output dimensions (profitability, valuation, growth) from an efficiency perspective — maximum output for a given level of input. A Data Envelopment Analysis calculates relative efficiency scores for firms from a linear programming model. Strength-Based Efficiency (SBE) scores for the chosen input and output measures are correlated with returns, and an SBE index is determined by finding the maximum correlation with returns over subsets of (input, output) measures. Edirisinghe *et al.* find a strong relationship between firm strength and stock returns. In the analysis it is found that market risk is largely independent of strength-based efficiency, so summarizing firm specific accounting information into an index, which is then part of a model for predicting returns, could be effective.

The objective defined by a utility function is a successful approach to studying financial decision making. The goals or investment targets are presented as constraints or requirements. Of course, goals are objectives, so an alternative approach is to include the goals in the objective. Geyer and Ziemba (2008) use a convex penalty for failure to meet goals in the objective. Browne (1999b) sets as an objective to maximize the probability of wealth exceeding that of a benchmark portfolio (index) by a predetermined amount. With the budget constraint excluding the shock term, the investment proportions x_t at time t, and the benchmark proportions π_t, the objective is

$$\max_x \{ \Pr[W(T, x) > (1 + \epsilon)W(T, \pi)] \}.$$

It is possible to set $(1 + \epsilon)W(T, \pi) = W_{VaR}$ and find a strategy which maximizes the probability of exceeding a deterministic target. Browne determines the probability maximizing investment strategy. In the case of a deterministic benchmark the strategy is equivalent to buying a European digital option with a particular strike and payoff (Browne, 1999a).

Even in the more general case of a stochastic benchmark, the optimal proportional strategy is composed of the benchmark and a hedging component. In comparisons with a stochastic benchmark, it is possible to set the benchmark as the Kelly portfolio, which maximizes the log of final wealth. The problem is then to find a portfolio which maximizes the probability of beating the Kelly. In the long run there is no such portfolio, but what about in the short run? Browne (2000) solves the probability maximizing problem for fixed T, finding a strategy that will beat the Kelly by an arbitrary $\epsilon\%$ with probability $\frac{1}{1+\epsilon}$.

The log utility is a special case of the Epstein–Zin function, where $\psi = \gamma = 1$. (Also the power utility as $\gamma \to 1$.) This is appropriate when the asset return dynamics are stationary, an assumption unlikely to hold in practice. When the objective is to maximize the logarithm of terminal wealth the strategy is the "optimal growth" policy. For a sequence of T investment periods starting with capital w_0, wealth at time T is $w_0 \prod_{t=1}^{T} R'(t)X(t) = w_0 \left(exp[\frac{1}{T} \sum_{t=1}^{T} \ln \left(R'(t)X(t) \right)] \right)^{T}$. So maximizing $\max_x E \ln[W(T)]$ optimizes the growth rate. In the continuous time format without the shocks, the objective is $\max_x \left\{ (\alpha - re)'X + r - \frac{1}{2}X'\Sigma X \right\}$. The strategy which maximizes the growth rate of capital has been termed the "Kelly" strategy (Kelly, 1956).

Although the Kelly strategy was developed from price dynamics determined by geometric Brownian motion (geometric random walk in discrete time), the dynamics, which include shocks can be accommodated. Assuming the shocks come in clusters based on market conditions, the time periods can be segmented into regimes. Then the price and wealth dynamics are defined by geometric Brownian motion within each regime, with the parameters being regime dependent. In this setup, the maximizing of $E \log W(T)$ is analytic (MacLean and Ziemba, 2013). It is reasonable to associate the Kelly strategy with the log utility and consider the type of strategy resulting from various constraints on decisions or wealth goals. Some of the results from considering variations on the log utility model are described in MacLean and Ziemba (2013). The risk and return properties of the Kelly are significant. In volatile markets or faced with parameter uncertainty, the investor can "back-off" the Kelly by using a fractional Kelly approach, where the size of the investment in risky assets is reduced but the proportions are maintained at the Kelly values.

Some of the strongest properties of the optimal growth strategy relate to its evolutionary performance in an equilibrium capital market. In a frictionless market (no transactions costs) Bahsoun *et al.* (2013) show that the Kelly rule is globally evolutionary stable, meaning that any other essentially different strategy will become extinct with probability 1. In a market with transactions costs Bahsoun *et al.* (2013) study optimal growth investment using the classical model of economic growth (Gale, 1956). They define "rapid growth" paths as ones which maximize the conditional expectation of the growth rate, and show that rapid growth paths are asymptotically optimal — no strategy can grow asymptotically faster.

If the utility of final wealth is the power function $U(W) = \frac{1}{1-\gamma}W^{1-\gamma}$, $\gamma > 0$, and the price dynamics are defined by geometric Brownian motion, then the optimal investment strategy is $x_\gamma = \frac{1}{\gamma}x^*$, where x^* is the Kelly strategy (Merton, 1971). When the geometric Brownian motion dynamics (and log-normality of returns distributions) do not apply, the strategy x_γ is not optimal.

Davis and Lleo (2013) consider a variety of alternative models for price dynamics and determine the strategy which maximizes $E\left[\frac{1}{1-\gamma}W(T)^{1-\gamma}\right]$. The first variation is an intertemporal asset pricing model, with the return rate depending linearly on state variables (factors). The optimal portfolio invests in a fractional Kelly portfolio and cash. The fractional Kelly fund is a blend of funds: a Kelly portfolio and an intertemporal hedging portfolio with weights $\frac{1}{\gamma}$ and $-\frac{1-\gamma}{\gamma}$, respectively. The Kelly portfolio is time dependent, having the form $\Sigma^{-1}(a + AF(t))$, for factors $F(t)$ at time t.

A variation on this case is where the observations on asset prices are filtered to obtain estimates of the return parameters and the state variable process. The portfolio which maximizes $E\left[\frac{1}{1-\gamma}W(T)^{1-\gamma}\right]$ is determined. Again the optimal portfolio allocates investment capital to a fractional Kelly portfolio and cash. The fractional Kelly portfolio is a blend of three funds: the Kelly portfolio (with return rate depending on the estimated state process); an intertemporal hedging portfolio; a partial observation portfolio. In the fractional Kelly portfolio, the weight on the Kelly portfolio is $\frac{1}{\gamma}$, and the combined weight in the other two is $-\frac{1-\gamma}{\gamma}$.

In another variation, Davis and Lleo consider a benchmark objective. Given the stochastic benchmark evolving from geometric Brownian motion with drift rate depending on factors, and the relative return $V(T) = \ln\left(\frac{W(T)}{I(T)}\right)$, they maximize $E\left[\frac{1}{1-\gamma}V(T)^{1-\gamma}\right]$. The resulting fractional Kelly portfolio is a blend of a Kelly portfolio (depending on the state variables through the drift), an intertemporal hedging portfolio and a benchmark tracking portfolio.

Davis and Lleo also consider the pricing model where the diffusion is augmented by shocks, defined by a homogeneous Poisson process. In a maximize $E\left[\frac{1}{1-\gamma}V(T)^{1-\gamma}\right]$ problem, they determine the optimal fractional Kelly portfolio as a mixture of a Kelly fund and an intertemporal hedging fund. The Kelly fund or log optimal portfolio is decomposed into a standard Kelly and a jump related portfolio. The weights in the components is more complicated, involving drift and jump terms.

The point in these variations on the asset price dynamics is that the log optimal or Kelly portfolio is a key component of the optimal solution. The solutions are fractional Kelly in the sense in that they "back-off" the Kelly by blending it with other safer portfolios.

Some calibration of the effect of reducing the investment in the Kelly portfolio using fractional strategies has been developed. MacLean *et al.* (2011) calculated wealth trajectories for fractional Kelly strategies under varying market scenarios. The capital growth of the full Kelly is impressive, but the downside losses are shown to be large in volatile markets. Scholz and Walther (2013) did a similar computational analysis, to study the effect of position sizing (fraction invested) on wealth accumulation. Their models are lognormal (geometric Brownian motion) and time varying returns in a first order autoregressive model (rate of return depending on state variables). Using a trading system based on the moving average, a fractional Kelly proportions strategy and a random positions strategy are employed when a trading signal is received. The results indicate that the final wealth is very much dependent on market conditions, as well as the measures of performance suggest that the trade-off between returns and risk from a fractional Kelly strategy is wisest for investors.

Davis and Lleo (2013) have shown that a model with shocks in the dynamics of returns and a power utility function of final wealth has an optimal portfolio strategy which has an option component. This is also true when the objective is maximizing the probability of beating a stochastic benchmark (Browne, 1999b). Thorp and Mizusawa (2013) consider the option component in two models for asset returns: log-normal, and fat tails (truncated "t"). Their interest is in the protection against losses provided by the option, so the strategies are a blend of stock and T-Bills versus the same blend of stock option and T-Bills. Even in the log-normal world, where the stock index optimizes growth, the impact of options in reducing maximum drawdowns is large. The advantages in using the option depend on parameter values: mean, variance, risk free return.

In the fat tails case the advantages of the option are clear. Both the geometric returns and the drawdowns favor the option portfolio. In some cases option portfolios are located on the mean-variance efficient frontier beyond any index portfolio. In addition they provide a better drawdown distribution. These numeric results are consistent with the optimality of the portfolio when stocks have extreme price dynamics. If the risk aversion parameter $1 - \gamma$ is lower, the weight on the option is higher.

Readings

Algoet, P. H. and Cover, T. M. (1988). Asymptotic optimality and asymptotic equipartition properties of log-optimum investment, *Annals of Probability*, **16**: 876–898.

Anoulova, S. V., Evstigneev, I. V. and Gundlach, V. M. (2000). Turnpike theorems for positive multivalued stochastic operators, *Advances in Mathematical Economics*, **2**: 1–20.

Barberis, N. (2000). Investing for the long run when returns are predictable, *Journal of Finance* **LV**(Feb): 225–264.

Bahsoun, W., Evstigneev, I. V. and Taksar, M. I. (2013). Growth-optimal investments and numeraire portfolios under transactions costs in *Handbook of the Fundamentals of Financial Decision Making*. Singapore: World Scientific, 789–809.

Browne, S. (1999a). Reaching goals by a deadline: Digital options and continuous-time active portfolio management, *Advances in Appllied Probability* **31**: 551–577.

Browne, S. (1999b). Beating a moving target: Optimal portfolio strategies for outperforming a stochastic benchmark, *Finance and Stochastics* **3**: 275–294.

Browne, S. (2000). Can you do better than Kelly in the short run? in *Finding the Edge: Mathematical Analysis of Casino Games*, Vancura, O., Cornelius, J., Eadington, W. R. (eds.). Institute for the Study of Gambling and Commercial Gaming: University of Nevada.

Campbell, J. Y., Chou, Y. I. and Viceira, L. (2003). A multivariate model of strategic asset allocation, *Journal of Financial Economics* **67**: 41–80.

Consigli, G., MacLean, L., Zhao, Y. and Ziemba, W. (2009). The bond-stock yield differential as a risk indicator in financial markets, *The Journal of Risk* **11**(3): 1–22.

Davis, M. and Lleo, S. (2013). Optimality of fractional Kelly strategies in *Handbook of the Fundamentals of Financial Decision Making*, MacLean, L. C. and Ziemba, W. T. (eds.). Singapore: World Scientific, 753–789.

Edirisinghe, C., Zhang, X. and Shyi, S.-C. (2013). DEA-based firm strengths and market efficiency in US and Japan, *Handbook of the Fundamentals of Financial Decision Making*, MacLean, L. C. and Ziemba, W. T. (eds.). Singapore: World Scientific, 611–637.

Fama, E. F. and French, F. (1992). The cross-section of expected stock returns, *Journal of Finance*, **47**(June): 427–466.

Gale, D. (1956). A closed linear model of production, in: *Linear Inequalities and Related Systems*. Kuhn, H. W. *et al.* (eds.), Princeton: Princeton University Press, 285–303.

Geyer, A. and Ziemba, W. T. (2008). The innovest Austrian pension fund planning model InnoALM, *Operations Research* **56**(4): 797–810.

Kelly, J. R. (1956). A new interpretation of the information rate, *Bell System Technical Journal* **35**: 917–926.

Ma, Y., MacLean, L., Xu, K. and Zhao, Y. (2011). A scenario-dependent market neutral strategy for sector select ETF's, *Pacific Journal of Optimization* **7**(2): 281–296.

MacLean, L., Thorp, E., Zhao, Y. and Ziemba, W. (2011). How does the *Fortune's Formula* — Kelly capital growth model perform? *Journal of Portfolio Management* **37**(4): 96–111.

MacLean, L. C. and Ziemba, W. T. (2013). The Kelly strategy for investing: Risk and reward in *Handbook of the Fundamentals of Financial Decision Making*, MacLean, L. C. and Ziemba, W. T. (eds.). Singapore: World Scientific, 637–683.

Merton, R. C. (1971). Optimum consumption and portfolio rules in a continuous-time model. *Journal of Economic Theory* **3**: 373–413.

Merton, R. C. (1973). An intertemporal capital asset pricing model, *Econometrica* **41**(5): 867–887.

Rosenberg, B., Reid, K. and Lanstein, R. (1985). Pervasive evidence of market inefficiency, *Journal of Portfolio Managment* **11**(3): 9–16.

Rubinov, A. M. (1980). *Superlinear Multivalued Mappings and their Applications to Problems of Mathematical Economics.* Leningrad: Nauka (in Russian).

Scholz, P. and Walther (2013). Managing position size depending on asset price characterstics, *Handbook of the Fundamentals of Financial Decision Making*, MacLean, L. C. and Ziemba, W. T. (eds.). Singapore: World Scientific.

Thorp, E. O. and Mizusawa, S. (2013). Maximizing capital growth with black swan protection in *Handbook of the Fundamentals of Financial Decision Making*, MacLean, L. C. and Ziemba, W. T. (eds.). Singapore: World Scientific, 849–873.

Ziemba, W. T. (2003). *The Stochastic Programming Approach to Asset Liability and Wealth Management, AIMR.*

Appendix F: Dynamic Pricing

Market dynamics

Assume that the economic situation is driven by a set of risk factors which include both micro and macro market indicators, such as realized stock and bond market returns, currency strength, market volatility indicators, corporate dividend yield, interest rate policies, yield spread and credit spread. Let F_t be the k-vector of these indicators at time t.

The dynamics of the factors characterize the dynamics of the financial market. It is assumed that the market is composed of epochs. Furthermore, the market states over time $\{S(t), t > 0\}$ follow a discrete state Markov process. The state space is finite: $S = \{S_1, \ldots, S_m\}$, and states will be referred to as regimes: $\{1, \ldots, m\}$, for the transition probability function between regimes is given by the matrix $P = (p_{ij})$. If the distribution over regimes at time t is $\pi(t) = (\pi_i(t), \ldots, \pi_m(t))$, then $\pi(t) = \pi(t-1)P$.

Given the Markov process for regimes, assume that the factors F_t follow a regime-switching vector autoregressive VAR(1) model. So within regime

$$F_t = \alpha_{S_t} + F_{t-1}\beta_{S_t} + \varepsilon_{S_t},$$

where α_{S_t} and β_{S_t} are regime-dependent coefficients and ε_{S_t} is an i.i.d. process with standard multivariate normal distribution having covariance Σ_{S_t}. Within a regime, i.e., a type of market, the factors are a stochastic dynamic process, where the dynamics of the factors are defined by a first order autoregressive model. The regimes follow a Markov process with the switching dynamics defined by the transition matrix P.

An important feature of the regime switching model is that the states/regimes and regime dependent parameters can be estimated from data on the factors. To describe the algorithm used to estimate a regime-switching model, we provide a generic version of the expectation-maximization algorithm. Let Θ be the set of parameters $\{\alpha_{S_t}, \beta_{S_t}, \Sigma_{S_t}, P\}$ for the model, X the sequence of observations of the factors $\{F_t\}$ over time, and Y the sequence of unobservable regimes $\{S_t\}$ over time. Denote $\mathcal{Y}$ the space of all possible regime sequences for the time period. The marginal maximum log-likelihood is expressed as:

$$\max_{\Theta} \left\{ \ln \left(\sum_{Y \in y} P(X, Y; \Theta) \right) \right\},$$

where $P(X, Y, \Theta)$ is the joint probability distribution function of X and Y.

An iterative algorithm can be designed as follows:

1. Set the number of regimes at m. This determines the number of parameters in the regime switching VAR(1) model.

2. E-step: Set an initial value θ_0 for the true parameter set Θ, calculate the conditional distribution function, $Q(Y) = P(Y|X; \Theta_0)$, and determine the expected log-likelihood, $E^Q[\ln P(X, Y; \Theta)]$.

3. M-step: Maximize the expected log-likelihood with respect to the conditional distribution of the hidden variable to obtain an improved estimate of Θ. The improved estimate is: $\Theta_1 = arg\max_\Theta\{E^Q[\ln P(X, Y; \Theta)]\}$.

4. With $\Theta_1\Theta$ as the new initial value for Θ, return to the E-Step.

In the E-step, given the observed data and current estimate of the parameter set, the hidden data are estimated using the conditional expectation. After estimating the parameters, a dynamic programming algorithm is applied to characterize the prevailing regime in each period by maximizing the joint probability of regimes given the observed data.

Discrete Time Asset Pricing Model

Consider a competitive financial market with n assets whose prices are stochastic dynamic processes. Let the vector of prices at time t be $P_t = (P_{0t}, \ldots, P_{nt})'$, where P_{0t} is the price of the risk-free asset, with rate of return r_t at time t. Let $Y_{it} = \ln(P_{it})i = 1, \ldots, n$ be the log-prices.

Model with Jumps

Consider that asset prices are identified at equally spaced points in time, $t = 1, \ldots, T$. Assume that the dynamics of price movements between times are defined by a geometric random walk with drift plus point processes. The idea with the point processes is to include the effect of market factors in the price dynamics. When the factors deviate substantially from benchmark values the asset prices react. The conditional price dynamics, given parameter values and initial values Y_{i0}, are defined by the equations for $i = 1, \ldots, n$ and $t = 1, \ldots, T$

$$Y_{it} = Y_{i0} + R_{i1} + \cdots + R_{it},$$

where for $s = 1, \ldots, t$

$$R_{is} = \left[\alpha_i + \sum_{j=1}^{n} \delta_{ij} Z_{js} \right] + \left[\sum_{j=1}^{k} \vartheta_{ijs} \Delta N_j(\lambda_{js}) \right].$$

In these equations, $Z_s = (Z_{1s}, \ldots, Z_{ns})', s = 1, \ldots, t$ are independent multivariate normal variables and $N_j(\lambda_j)$ are counting processes with intensities $\lambda_j, j = 1, \ldots, k$. As the deviations on factors increase the chance of a jump driven by the factor indices increases, with a high probability of a jump in the regimes with extreme (beyond the thresholds) scores.

The parameters $\vartheta_{ijs}, j = 1, \ldots, k$ are independent random variables capturing the size of the jumps to asset prices, and it is assumed they also depend on the deviation in factors. To have the jump size reflecting extreme returns, it is assumed that size at time t depends linearly on the factor deviations ψ_{js}. If there is a shock at time s, the size is assumed to be

$$\vartheta_{ijs} = \varphi_{ij} + \theta_{ij} \psi_{js} + \eta_i W_{is},$$

where W_{is} are independent, standard Gaussian variables. The sign of ψ determines the direction of the jump (*UP* or *DOWN*).

The counting processes augment the random walk, generating more extreme price movements. If the intensities are such that jumps occur in clusters of the same type (*UP* or *DOWN*), then the trajectory of cumulative price movements drifts away from the random walk. If the deviations are in opposite directions then the jumps could cancel, and then dynamics would be closer to the random walk. It is instructive, therefore, to consider the effect of the point processes in the regions/regimes defined by the factors. In doing so, let $\Delta N_j(\lambda_{js}) = 0$ below the thresholds and $\Delta N_j(\lambda_{js}) = 1$ above the thresholds. Then in Regime m,

$$R_{ism} = \left[\alpha_{im} + \sum_{j=1}^{n} \delta_{ijm} Z_{js} \right] + \left[\sum_{j=1}^{k} [\varphi_{ijm} + \theta_{ijm} \psi_{js} + \eta_{im} W_{is}] \right].$$

If the deviation in factor indices is written in terms of the factors, the return model has the matrix form

$$R_s = A_m + F_s B_m + \Gamma_m \epsilon.$$

Although the components are combined above, the separation into a random walk and non-homogenous point process is important to understanding market forces. Furthermore it is possible to separate the components in the estimation.

It is important to note that the predicted prices in the next period are the basis of investment decisions for that period. The regime switching VAR(1) model is used to forecast $\hat{F}_s$, one period ahead factors, from observations on $\hat{F}_{s-1}$. Then the predicted returns are linear functions of $\hat{F}_s$.

Model with Regimes

The consolidation of the pricing model with random walk and jump components into a linear factor model establishes the setup for a regime based model. Having presented a regime-switching model for risk factors, it is assumed that returns of all primary investment assets follow a linear model with regime-dependent risk sensitivity. Our interest is in developing a predictive model for asset returns based on the forecast of the risk factors. Explicitly, the following structure is specified:

$$R_t = A_{S_t} + \hat{F}_t B_{S_t} + \Gamma_{S_t} \epsilon.$$

Given the predicted factor and the state at time t, the one-period return vector is conditionally multivariate normal with conditional mean return vector and covariance matrix as

$$\mu_{S_t} = A_{S_t} + \hat{F}_t B_{S_t},$$

$$\sum_{S_t} = \Gamma_{S_t} \Gamma'_{S_t}.$$

Unlike conventional random walk/Brownian models, this model provides time-varying and state-dependent returns driven by risk factors.

Investment Model

The investment decisions are the fractions of capital to allocate to n risky investment opportunities. Consider that the decision points are made at discrete time points $t_1 = 0, t_2 = t_1 + d, \ldots, t_{L+1} = t_L + d = T$. An investment strategy is the vector process: $\{(x_0(t_l), X(t_l)), l = 1, \ldots, L\} = \{(x_0(t_l), x_1(t_l), \ldots, x_n(t_l)), l = 1, \ldots, L\}$, where $\sum_{i=0}^{n} x_i(t_l) = 1$ for any t_l, with $x_0(t_l)$ the investment fraction in the risk-free asset and $x_i(t_l)$ the fraction invested in risky asset $i, i = 1, \ldots, n$.

The change in wealth from an investment decision $X(t)$ is determined by the changes in prices. Let the vector of prices at time t be $P(t) = (P_0(t), P_1(t), \ldots, P_n(t))'$, where $P_0(t)$ is the price of the risk-free asset, with rate of return r_t at time t.

Let $Y_i(t) = \ln P_i(t), i = 0, \ldots, n$, be the log-prices. The price dynamics are defined by the stochastic differential equations: $dY_0(t) = r_t dt$, $dY(t) = \alpha dt + \Delta dZ$, with $Y(t) = (Y_1(t), \ldots, Y_n(t))', \alpha = (\alpha_1, \ldots, \alpha_n)', \Delta = (\delta_{ij}), dZ = (dZ_1, \ldots, dZ_n)'$, where $dZ_i, i = 1, \ldots, n$ are independent Brownian motions.

Let $\Sigma^2 = \Sigma'\Sigma$, and $\varphi = \alpha + \frac{1}{2}\Sigma^2 e$. Then the instantaneous change in wealth is

$$dW(t) = [X'(t)(\varphi - re) + r]W(t)dt + W(t)[X'(t)\Sigma dZ].$$

If the wealth at time t is w_t and the investment decision is maintained through rebalancing as a fixed fraction from time t to time $t+1$, then the accumulated wealth is

$$W(t+1)$$
$$= w_t \cdot exp\left\{\left[X'(t)(\varphi - re) + r - \frac{1}{2}X'(t)\Sigma^2 X(t)\right] + X(t)'\Sigma Z\right\},$$

where $Z' = (Z_1, \ldots, Z_n), Z_i \sim N(0,1)$.

The wealth equation can be extended to the case of regimes. The conditional wealth at the end of period t if the regime is k, given the fixed investment strategy (t), is

$W_k(t+1) = w_t \cdot exp\{[X'(t)(\varphi_k - re) + r - \frac{1}{2}X'(t)\Sigma_k^2 X(t)] + X(t)'\Sigma_k Z\}$. The rate of return in regime k is $R_k(X(t)) = lnW_k(t+1) - lnw_t = \{[X'(t)(\varphi_k - re) + r - \frac{1}{2}X'(t)\Sigma_k^2 X(t)] + X(t)'\Sigma_k Z\}$, which has a multivariate normal distribution.

Assume that the distribution over regimes is

$$\pi(t) = (\pi_1(t), \ldots, \pi_m(t)).$$

Let the density for $R_k(X(t))$ be denoted by $f_k(v|t), k = 1, \ldots, m$. If the unconditional rate of return on investment $X(t)$ is $R(X(t))$, then the unconditional distribution for $R(X(t))$ is a mixture of normals $f(v|t) = \pi_1(t)f_1(v|t) + \cdots + \pi_m(t)f_m(v|t)$.

The wealth equation for the investment strategy $X = \{X(t), t = 1, \ldots, T\}$ is the basis for the decision model:

$$\max_X u(W(T))$$

subject to

$$W_k(t+1) = w_t \cdot exp\left\{\left[X'(t)(\varphi_k - re) + r - \frac{1}{2}X'(t)\Sigma_k^2 X(t)\right]\right.$$
$$\left. +X(t)'\Sigma_k Z\right\}, \quad k = 1, \ldots, m.$$
$$X'(t) \cdot e = 1, t = 1, \ldots, T-1.$$

Optimal Control

Although the price and wealth dynamics are written as continuous functions of time in the above model, the decision $X(t)$ is made at discrete time points and assumed fixed between those points. This has the effect of making the dynamics a geometric random walk. Even with jumps in a point process, the jumps are aggregated in a time interval generating regimes with geometric random walk dynamics within regime.

If the investment decision $X(t)$ is a continuous function of time then the wealth dynamics follow a continuous time stochastic process.

In the case of geometric Brownian motion price movements, the wealth dynamics are

$$dW(t) = [X'(t)(\varphi - re) + r]W(t)dt + W(t)[X'(t)\Sigma dZ].$$

If there is a Poisson jump process then the accumulated jumps augment the wealth dynamics

$$dW(t) = [X'(t)(\varphi - re) + r]W(t)dt + W(t)[X'(t)\Sigma dZ]$$
$$+ \int_Z X'(t)\eta(z)Q(dt, dz),$$

where $Q(dt, dz)$ is a probability measure for a stationary Poisson process on Z, and $\eta(z)$ is a random jump size vector.

The objective is to maximize over the continuous function $X(t)$, the expected utility of terminal wealth over the time horizon T

$$\max_X E[u(W(T))].$$

It is reasonable to approach the control problem by discretizing time and solving the approximating problem.

In the control setting define the value function

$$\Phi(t, w) = \max_X E[u(W_T^{t,w})], (t, w) \in [0, T] \times (0, \infty).$$

Then the optimal control satisfies the Hamilton–Jacobi–Bellman (HJB) partial differential equation

$$\frac{\partial \Phi}{\partial t} + \max_X \left[w[X'(t)(\varphi - re) + r]'\lambda + \frac{1}{2}w^2 tr(X'(t)\Sigma\Sigma'X(t)D^2\Phi \right],$$

subject to the boundary condition

$$\Phi(T, w) = u(w).$$

For case of a power utility, $(w) = \frac{w^\gamma}{\gamma}$, the HJB equation has an explicit solution. In general dynamic programming techniques are used to obtain numerical solutions.

Section F Exercises

[F1] (a) Develop a generalization of the model considered in the Bahsoun, Evstigneev and Taksar paper in the Handbook, allowing for (restricted) short sales of assets. Extend the capital growth theory presented in the paper to this model, assuming that the set of admissible portfolio vectors at date t is given by some cone $K_t(s^t) \supseteq R_+^n$.

(b) Consider the special case of polyhedral cones $K_t(s^t)$, including the main example of $K_t(s^t)$ defined by margin requirements. Try to deduce the theory of growth optimal investments in the case of polyhedral $K_t(s^t)$ from that presented in the paper where $K_t(s^t) = R_+^n$.

[F2] What functionals $F_t(x_{t-1}, s^t, \cdot)$ have to be maximized in order to recursively generate an infinite rapid path (x_t) by the formula $x_t \in arg\max F_t(x_{t-1}, s^t,)$? Try to approach this question by using the idea of *efficient functionals* (Rubinov, 1980) in the deterministic von Neumann–Gale model. To begin with, examine this problem in the case of a stationary or a Markov model.

[F3] (a) Design methods for computing growth optimal investment strategies (rapid paths) based on the *turnpike principle*. To this end extend the turnpike theorems by Anoulova *et al.* (2000) to the case of polyhedral, transition cones G_t, which are not necessarily strictly convex.

(b) Examine whether the assumption of strict convexity of G_t can be replaced by appropriate assumptions of nondegeneracy of the underlying probability distributions (similar to those guaranteeing the uniqueness of the growth optimal portfolio in Algoet and Cover, 1988).

[F4] (a) Develop a Markov version of the theory of growth-optimal investments under transaction costs. Assuming that the von Neumann–Gale investment model is Markov, i.e., the process s_t is Markov and the transition cones $G_t(s_t)$ depend only on s_t, show that among all infinite rapid paths with the given initial state there exists at least one possessing a (properly defined) Markov property. To obtain such a Markov sufficiency theorem, try to employ the methods of stochastic control over an infinite time horizon that do not rely upon the Bellman principle of dynamic programming, which is directly applicable only in the finite horizon case.

[F5] Refer to the Mizusawa and Thorp paper in the Handbook. Consider the option strategy $K = 0.9, f = 0.2$.

(a) What is the Black–Scholes price of the call, C?

(b) How many calls does $f = 0.2$ buy?

(c) How much is invested in T-bills?

(d) Using equation (4), to what extent can we replace calls plus T-bills by puts plus the index, without borrowing?

[F6] Assuming there are no transactions costs and no borrowing or lending limits, how might you exploit the following situations. Explain your answers.

(a) The left side of equation (4) is greater than the right side.

(b) The left side is less than the right side.

(c) How would you use a price difference between the two sides of equation (4), plus the result of exercise 1(d) to more advantageously apply the strategy?

[F7] Assuming equation (4) holds, when can one completely replace calls by puts (plus the index) without borrowing?

[F8] In what ways do you think the log-normal distribution for stock index returns differs from real data?

[**F9**] If you use American options (exercisable anytime) instead of European options (exercisable only at expiration), how would you deal with early exercise in practice?

[**F10**] The smallest calendar year wealth relative for the S&P 500 index over the 86-year-period, 1926–2011, was 0.5666, occurring in 1931.

    (a) For 86 index independent draws from the log-normal distribution in part I, what is the probability the minimum wealth relative is this small or smaller?

    (b) Repeat using the truncated t distribution of part II.

[**F11**] Consider an investor whose preference for consumption over two periods is represented by the cardinal utility function $u(c_1, c_2)$. Suppose that his preference ordering is *mutually utility independent* — preference ordering on c_2 is independent of the level on c_1 and vice versa.

    (a) Show that $u(c_1, c_2)$ may be represented as

$$u(c_1, c_2) = a_1(c_2) + b_1(c_2)u(c_1, c_2^0)$$

    and

$$u(c_1, c_2) = a_2(c_1) + b_2(c_1)u(c_1^0, c_2),$$

    for fixed but arbitrary c_1^0, c_2^0.

    (b) Show that u may be represented as

$$u(c_1, c_2) = f_1(c_1) + f_2(c_2) + kf_1(c_1)f_2(c_2).$$

    (c) If $k > 0$, show that the investor's utility function may be transformed into the equivalent form

$$u(c_1, c_2) = g_1(c_1)g_2(c_2).$$

    (d) Show that $u(c_1, c_2)$ is concave in c_1, for any fixed c_2, and concave in c_2 for any fixed c_1, if f_1, f_2 are non-negative concave functions and $k \geq 0$.

    (e) Give an example of a function u with $u(c_1, c_2) = f_1(c_1) + f_2(c_2) + kf_1(c_1)f_2(c_2)$, in which f_1, f_2 are positive, strictly increasing, strictly concave functions and $k \geq 0$, but $u(c_1, c_2)$ is not concave on R^2.

(f) Give an example of a function u, with $u(c_1, c_2) = f_1(c_1) + f_2(c_2) + k f_1(c_1) f_2(c_2)$, strictly increasing, strictly concave in c_1 and c_2 separately, for which there exists a gamble in which c_1 and c_2 are correlated which is preferred to the status quo.

[F12] (Interest rates and bond prices: deterministic case) Let ρ_t be the instantaneous (one-period) interest at time $t = 0, 1, \ldots, T$. Let $R(t)$ be the long-term interest rate over the interval $[t, T]$ (i.e., the effective constant one-period interest rate applying in the interval $[t, T]$) Assume that ρ_t is known with certainty.

(a) Using arbitrage arguments in perfect capital markets, show that

$$[1 + R(t)]^{T-t} = \prod_{t=t}^{T} (1 + \rho_t).$$

(b) In the continuous time limit show that (a) becomes

$$R(t) = (T - t)^{-1} \int_t^T \rho_\tau d\tau.$$

$$p'(t) - \rho(t)p(t) = -r, \quad \text{and} \quad p(T) = 1.$$

Suppose a bond of par value \$1, time to maturity T, and (continuous) coupon rate r is issued at time $t = 0$. Let $p(t)$ be market value of the bond at time t.

(c) Show that $p(t)$ satisfies the differential equation

$$p'(t) - \rho(t)p(t) = -r \quad \text{and} \quad p(T) = 1.$$

(d) Show that

$$p(t) = \exp(-(T - t)R(t)) \left[1 + r \int_t^T \exp((T - t)R(\tau)d\tau \right].$$

Consider the special case in which $\rho(t)$ is linearly strictly decreasing and ≥ 0 in $[0, T]$, and suppose that $R(0) = r$. Suppose also that $\rho(0) = 1$; that is, the bonds are issued at par.

(e) Show that $p(t)$ is strictly increasing in some closed interval $[0, t_1]$, $t_1 > 0$, and strictly decreasing in some closed interval $[t_2, T], t_2 < T$.

(f) Show that any stationary point of $p(t)$ must be a strict local maximum of $p(\cdot)$.

(g) Show that $p(\cdot)$ has one and only one stationary point in $(0, T)$, and this point is the unique global maximum of $p(\cdot)$ in $[0, T]$. Let this point be t_m.

   (i) If $p''(0) \leq 0$ show that $p''(t) < 0$ for all $t \in (0, T)$.
   (ii) If $p''(0) > 0$, show that there exists a $t_0 \in (0, t_m)$ such that $p(\cdot)$ is strictly increasing and strictly convex in $(0, t_0)$, and strictly concave in $(t_0, T]$.

$$W_t = (1 + f)^v (1 - f)^{t-v} W_0,$$

if he wins v of his bets.

(h) Show that $G = p \log(1 + f) + q \log(1 - f)$.

(i) Interpret this result in terms of expected utility theory.

(j) Show that the optimal bet is

$$f^* = p - q \quad \text{and} \quad G^* = p \log p + q \log q > 0.$$

(k) Interpret f^*, G^*.

(l) Calculate f^*, G^* if there is a tie with probability $r > 0$.

(m) Show there is no stationary sequence $\{f_1, f_2, \ldots, \}$ which is superior to $\{f^*, f^*, \ldots\}$.

[**F13**] (The Kelly criterion)

A gambler makes repeated bets in sequence against an infinitely rich adversary. At time t his wager is β_t dollars out of with his total wealth W_t. Suppose that the game is stationary and favorable, the probability of winning and losing being

$p > \frac{1}{2}$ and $q = 1 - p$, respectively. Suppose that the objective is to maximize the exponential rate of growth of W_t, namely,

$$G == \lim_{t \to \infty} (1/t) log(W_t/W_0),$$

where W_0 is the gambler's initial wealth. Assume that the gambler bets a constant fraction f of his capital in each period so $\beta_t = fW_t$.

(a) Show that in each period t the gambler's wealth is

$$W_t = (1 + f)^v (1 - f)^{t-v} W_0$$

if he wins v of his bets.

(b) Show that $G = p \log(1 + f) + q \log(1 - f)$.

(c) Interpret this result in terms of expected utility theory.

(d) Show that the optimal bet is

$$f^* = p - q \quad \text{and} \quad G^* = p \log p + q \log q > 0.$$

(e) Interpret f^*, G^*.

(f) Calculate f^*, G^* if there is a tie with probability $r > 0$.

(g) Show there is no stationary sequence $\{f_1, f_2, \ldots\}$ which is superior to $\{f^*, f^*, \ldots\}$.

[F14] (Definition of a martingale)

Suppose a sequence of random variables $\{X_i, i = 1, 2, \ldots\}$, has the property that $E|X_i| < \infty$ for all i. Then if $E(X_{n+1}|X_n, \ldots, X_1) = X_n$ a.e. for all n, the sequence is said to be a martingale. If $E(X_{n+1}|X_n, \ldots, X_1) \geq (\leq)X_n$ a.e. for all n, it is said to be a sub-martingale (super-martingale).

(a) Consider the game of roulette in which 38 numbers are equally likely, 18 of which are red, 18 are black, and 2 are green. Suppose a player utilizes the following strategy:

Step 1: Bet $1 on black.

Step 2: If black occurs go to 1. If red or green occurs go to 3.

Step 3: Go to step 1 but bet double the previous bet.

Let S_n be his winnings after play. Is S_n a martingale or sub- or super-martingale?

(b) More generally, let $\{X_n\}$ be a sequence of random variables where $\Pr[X_n = +1] = p \geq 0$ and $\Pr[X_n = -1] = 1 - p \geq 0$, respectively. Suppose on the nth trial we bet $B_n = f(X_1, \ldots, X_{n-1})$ and we receive $2B_n$ if $X_n = +1$ and zero if $X_n = -1$. Let $W_0 > 0$ be our initial fortune and S_n be the fortune after n plays. Is S_n a martingale, sub- or super-martingale?

[F15] This problem concerns the effect of uncertainty on savings decisions when the consumer has uncertainty concerning either his future income or his yield on capital investments.

Suppose that the consumer's utility function over present and future consumption C_1, C_2 is $u(C_1, C_2)$ where u is strictly monotone, concave and three times continuously differentiable. Consider the risk-aversion function,

$$\frac{2}{h^2}p = \frac{-u_{22}(C_1, C_2)}{u_2(C_1, C_2)},$$

for equally likely gambles $(C_1, C_2 - h)$ and $(C_1, C_2 + h)$, where $p > 0$ is the risk premium. Assume that the risk-aversion function is increasing in C_1 and decreasing in C_2; that is, decreasing temporal risk aversion.

(a) Graphically interpret the concept of decreasing temporal risk aversion.

(b) Suppose the consumer is endowed with consumption (C_1, C_2) and is offered a gamble having outcomes $\pm h$ of future consumption. Show that the consumer will accept the gamble only when the probability of a gain h say $\pi(h)$, is greater than $1/2$.

(c) Show that π is an increasing function of C_1.

(d) Show that π will fall with a simultaneous increase in C_2 and decrease in C_1.

Consider first the effects of uncertainty regarding the consumer's future income. His first-period budget constraint is $Y_1 = C_1 + S_1$, where Y_1 is his (certain) income in period 1 and S_1 is savings. Future consumption is $C_2 = Y_2 + S_1(1+r)$, where r is the rate of interest, assumed to be known in the case of pure income risk, and Y_2 is the uncertain income in period 2.

(e) Show that expected utility is

$$EU = \int u(C_1, Y_2) + (Y_1 - C_1)(1+r)dF(Y_2).$$

(f) Show that the first order and second order conditions for an optimal choice are

$E[U_1 - (1+r)U_2] = 0$ and $D = E[U_{11} - 2(1+r)U_{12} + (1+r)^2 U_{22}] < 0$, respectively.

(g) Verify $D < 0$.

(h) Show that the effect of an increase in present income is

$$\frac{\partial C_1}{\partial Y_1} = -\frac{(1+r)E[U_{12} - (1+r)U_{22}]}{D}.$$

(i) Assume that $\frac{\partial C_1}{\partial Y_1}$ is always positive. Show that this means that both present and future consumption are not inferior goods.

Write future income as $\gamma Y_2 + \theta$, where γ and θ are multiplicative and additive shift factors, respectively.

(j) Interpret the meaning of the two types of shift parameters.

Since $Y_2 \geq 0$ a multiplicative shift around zero will increase the mean. Hence to maintain a constant expected value, the additive shift must be negative. Taking the differential, the requirement is that $\frac{d\theta}{d\gamma} = -E[Y_2] \equiv -\phi$.

(k) Show that

$$\left(\frac{\partial C_1}{\partial \gamma}\right)_{\frac{\partial \theta}{\partial \gamma}=-\phi} = -\left(\frac{1}{D}\right)E[(U_{12}-(1+r)U_{22})(Y_2-\phi)].$$

(l) Show that decreasing temporal risk aversion is sufficient for the expression above to be <0. Hence increased uncertainty about future income increases savings.

Consider the case of capital risk. Suppose that in the first period the consumer can allocate his resources (Y_1) between present consumption (C_1) and capital investment K. Capital investment is transformed into resources available for future consumption by the function $f(K,\xi)$, where ξ is random. Consider the simple form $C_2 = K\xi$, where $\xi \geq 0$.

(m) Show that expected utility is $EU = \int U(C_1,(Y_1 - C_1)\xi)dF(\xi)$.

(n) Show that necessary and sufficient for a maximum of EU are $E[U_1 - \xi U_2] = 0$ and $H = E[U_{11} - 2\xi U_{12} + \xi^2 U_{22}] < 0$. Let the yield on capital be $\gamma(\xi-1)+\theta$. For a multiplicative shift around zero to keep the mean constant we must have

$$\frac{d\theta}{\partial \gamma} = -E[\xi - 1] \equiv= \mu.$$

(o) Show that

$$\left(\frac{\partial C_1}{\partial \gamma}\right)_{\frac{\partial \theta}{\partial \gamma}=-\mu} = -\left(\frac{1}{H}\right)KE[(U_{12}-\xi U_{22})(\xi - \mu)]$$
$$+ \frac{1}{H}E[U_2(\xi - \mu)].$$

[Differentiate the first-order conditions with respect to γ and evaluate the derivative at $(\gamma,0) = (1,0)$]. We refer to the first term as the income effect and the second term as the substitution effect.

(p) Show that the existence of risk aversion, i.e., U is concave, is a necessary and sufficient condition for the substitution effect to be positive. Show that the additional assumption of decreasing temporal risk aversion is sufficient for the income effect to be negative. Hence the total effect is ambiguous without further assumptions.

$$Z_n = \max_{x \in K} E_\xi u[f(x, \xi)]\xi.$$

[**F16**] This problem concerns the development of relatively easily computable upper and lower bounds on the value of information in uncertain decision problems. Suppose that a decision maker must choose a decision vector x from a constraint set K. A choice x will provide him with the payoff $f(x, \xi)$, where ξ is a random vector distributed independently of x. Assume that the decision maker knows the distribution function of ξ and that his utility function is u. If the decision must be made before ξ is observed, then the decision maker achieves maximum expected utility by solving

$$Z_n = \max_{x \in K} E_\xi u[f(x, \xi)],$$

Now if a clairvoyant were to tell the decision maker the precise realization of ξ that will occur before the decision x must be chosen then the decision maker's maximum expected utility would be

$$Z_p = \max_{x \in K} u[f(x, \xi)].$$

(a) Show that $Z_p \geq Z_n$.

Define the value of information V as the solution to

$$E_\xi \max_{x \in K} u[f(x, \xi) - V] = \max_{x \in K} E_\xi u[f(x, \xi)].$$

Thus, V is the cost which would equate the attainable expected utility with and without perfect information.

Assume that u is strictly increasing and that all relevant expectations and maxima exist.

(b) Show that $V \geq 0$. [Hint: Show that the assumption that $V < 0$ leads to a contradiction.]

(c) Let $V(x) \equiv h([a_1(x), \dots, a_m(x)]$ where $V : C \to R, h: R^m \to R, a_i : C \to R, i = 1, \dots, m$ and $C \subset R^m$ is a convex set. Show that V is concave idf h is concave and non-decreasing and the a_i are concave.

(d) Suppose that u is concave on R and f is concave on the convex set $K \times \Xi$, where Ξ is the domain of ξ. Show that $\leq C_1 \leq C_2$, where

$$C_i = \max_{x \in K} f(x\Xi, \bar{\xi}) - u^{-1}(c_i), i = 1, 2,$$

$$C_1 \equiv \max_{x \in K} E_\xi u[f(x, \xi)], c_2 \equiv E_\xi u[f(\bar{x}, \xi)],$$

where $\bar{x}$ solves $\max_{x \in K} f(x, \bar{\xi})$.

(e) Discuss the computational aspects of these bounds.

(f) Suppose the utility function takes the linear form $u(w) = aw + b, a > 0$. Show that

$$\frac{V}{a} = E_\xi \max_{x \in k} f(x, \xi) - \max_{x \in K} E_\xi f(x, \xi).$$

(g) Lt $v(x) = \max_{y \in D(x)} w(x, y)$ where $w : C \times D \to\to R, v : C \to R$, with $C \subset R^n$ and $D(\cdot) \subset R^l$ being convex sets. Suppose that for each $x \in C$ the maximum is attained for some $y_0(x) \in D(x)$. Show that v is a concave function of x if w is a concave function of (x, y).

(h) Let $a = 1$. Suppose that f is concave on the convex set $K \times \Xi$. Show that $V \leq f(\bar{x}, \bar{\xi}) - E_\xi f(\bar{x}, \xi) \equiv A$.

(i) Show that

$$V \leq \max_{x \in K} [f(\bar{x}, \tilde{\xi}) + \nabla f(x, \tilde{\xi})'(\bar{\xi} - \tilde{\xi})] - E_\xi f(\bar{x}, \xi) \equiv B,$$

where $\tilde{\xi}$ is any $\xi \in \Xi, \nabla f$ is the gradient vector, and $\tilde{x}$ solves $\max_{x \in K} f(x, \tilde{\xi})$.

(j) Show $A \leq B$.

(k) Discuss the computational aspects of the bounds A and B.

[F17] This problem is concerned with the effect of uncertainty on the savings-consumption-portfolio decision of an expected utility-maximizing investor faced with a two-period horizon.

(a) Suppose that the investor wishes to maximize $Eu(\theta, \alpha)$ with respect to the decision variable α, where θ is a random variable. Show that the first- and second-order conditions for a unique maximum α^* to exist are $Eu_\alpha(\theta, \alpha) = 0$ and $Eu_{\alpha\alpha}(\theta, \alpha) < 0$ (subscripts denote differentiation), assuming that the appropriate integrals are well behaved.

(b) Show that α^* (increases, is constant, decreases) if $u_\alpha(\theta, \alpha)$ is a (concave, linear, convex) function of α when the risk of θ is increased.

Suppose there are two periods, present and future. Let initial wealth be W and s be the savings rate; then consumption in the present period is $C = (1 - s)W$. Suppose r is the riskfree (gross) rate of interest and that the individual will receive the random bequest Y at the end of the present period. Assuming that utility is stationary and additive and that $0 < \beta < 1$ is a discount factor, the problem is to $\max_{0 \le s \le 1}\{u[(1 - s)W] + \beta Eu(Y + rsW)\}$.

(c) Determine when there will be an interior maximum.

(d) Develop the first- and second-order conditions assuming that there is an interior maximum.

(e) Show that the marginal propensity to save with respect to wealth is between 0 and 1. What happens if $s* = 0$ or 1?

(f) Show that if u' is a convex (concave) function of consumption, that is, $u'' > 0$ (<0), the investor will increase (decrease) his savings rate when there is increased uncertainty regarding his future income.

(g) Show that $u'' > 0$ for all utility functions displaying decreasing absolute risk aversion.

(h) Show that the investor will increase savings with increasing income uncertainty for the utility functions $\frac{1}{1-\alpha}C^{1-\alpha}, \log C$, and $-\phi^{-\gamma C}$.

Suppose now that the investor derives all his income from wealth that is, $Y \equiv 0$, but that the rate of return on wealth, r, is random.

(i) Show that increasing risk in r increases (decreases) savings if $2u''(C) + Cu''(C) > (<)0$.

(j) Show that increased risk increases (decreases) savings if $\alpha > 1(< 1)$ when $u(C) = \frac{1}{1-\alpha}C^{1-\alpha}$.

(k) Investigate the case when both r and Y are random.

Suppose now that the investor derives all his income from his return on wealth (i.e., $Y \equiv 0$) but that he may allocate his investment between two investments. Let δ and $1 - \delta$ be the proportions invested in assets 1 and 2 that have random (gross) rates of return r_1 and r_2, respectively.

(l) Suppose that $u' > 0$ and $u'' < 0$. Show that it is not possible to determine if it is advisable to reduce the proportion invested in an asset that becomes riskier.

(m) Suppose $u(C) = \frac{1}{1-\alpha}C^{1-\alpha}$ and $\alpha < 1$. Show that the optimal savings rate and the optimal proportion invested in asset 1 are decreased with an increase in the variability of r_1.

(n) Show that the result is ambiguous if $\alpha > 1$.

(o) What happens if $\alpha = 1$?

[**F18**] (Elementary properties of renewal processes)

Let $\{X_j, j = 1, 2, \ldots\}$ be a sequence of non-negative i.i.d. random variables with distribution F, such that $P[X_j = 0] < 1$. Let $\mu = EX$ (which exists, but may be ∞). Define $S_0 = 0$, $S_n = \sum_{j=1}^{n} X_j, n \geq 1$, and define $N(t) = sup\{n|S_n \leq t\}$. The stochastic process $\{N(t), t \geq O\}$ is called a renewal process. Intuitively, the X_n are "interarrival times" of some probabilistic process, and $N(t)$ is the number of "arrivals" in $[0, t]$.

(a) Show that $\frac{S_n}{n} \to \mu$ w.p. 1. as $n \to \infty$, and $N(t) < \infty$ w.p. 1.

  Show that $\lim_{t \to \infty} \frac{N(t)}{t} = \frac{1}{\mu}$ w.p. 1.

(b) Show that $\lim_{t \to \infty} \frac{N(t)}{t} = \frac{1}{\mu}$ w.p. 1.

  Suppose that a reward is earned by the renewal process. Let $Y(t)$ be the total reward earned by time t, and Y_n the incremental reward earned at the nth renewal. Assume that EX_n and EY_n are finite, and that the pairs (X_n, Y_n) are i.i.d.

  Assume temporarily that $Y_n \geq 0$ and $Y(t) \geq 0$ is non-decreasing in t.

(c) Show that

$$\sum_{n=1}^{N(t)} \frac{Y_n}{t} \to \frac{EY_1}{EX_1} \quad \text{w.p. 1 as } t \to \infty.$$

(d) Show that

$$\frac{Y_{N(t)+1}}{t} \to 0 \quad \text{w.p. 1 as } t \to \infty.$$

(e) Show that

$$\frac{Y(t)}{t} \to \frac{EY_1}{EX_1} \quad \text{w.p. 1 as } t \to \infty.$$

(f) Prove (e) when Y_n and $Y(t)$ are not restricted in sign.

  A simple but important generalization of the results above pertains to delayed renewal processes. Let $\{X_n, n = 1, \ldots\}$ be non-negative independent random variables such that X_1 has distribution G and $X_2, X_3, \ldots$ have the common distribution F, $EX_2 = \mu$. Let

$$S_0 = 0, S_n = \sum_{k=1}^{n} X_k, n \geq 1, \quad \text{and}$$

$$N_D(t) = \sup\{n | S_n \leq t\}.$$

The process $\{N_D(t), t \geq 0\}$ is a delayed renewal process.

(g) Show that

$$\frac{N_D(t)}{t} \to \frac{1}{\mu} \text{ w.p. 1 as } t \to \infty.$$

(h) Formulate and prove results similar to (e) and (f) for delayed renewal processes.

[**F19**] Consider an investor whose utility for lifetime consumption is $u(c_0, c_1, \ldots, c_T)$. For each i, suppose the elasticity of marginal utility of c_i is constant and equal to $\gamma_i - 1$.

(a) Show that for all i

$$u(c_0, c_1, \ldots, c_T) = \begin{matrix} a_i + b_i c^{\gamma_i} \text{ if } \gamma_i \neq 0 \\ a_i + b_i \log c_i \text{ if } \gamma_i = 0, \end{matrix}$$

where a_i, b_i are independent of c_i (but may be functions of $c_j, j \neq i$).

(b) Show that

$$u = a + b \prod_{i=0}^{T} c_i^{\gamma_i} \text{ or } u = a + b \log \prod_{i=0}^{T} c_i^{\gamma_i} \text{ for constants } a, b.$$

Assume that marginal utility of consumption is strictly positive for all i.

(c) Show that all γ_i must have the same sign, and $\gamma_i \cdot b > 0$.

(d) Show that a necessary and sufficient condition for strict concavity of u is

$$\sum_{i=0}^{T} \gamma_i < 1.$$

Suppose that γ_i reflect a constant rate of impatience between successive periods: $\gamma_i = \gamma \alpha^i$ for all i, where $\alpha \in (0, 1)$ is the impatience factor. By a linear transformation of the utility index, u may thus be chosen as

$$u = \delta \prod_{t=0}^{T} c_i^{\gamma \alpha^i} \text{ where } \delta = \begin{cases} 1 \text{ if } \gamma > 0 \\ -1 \text{ if } \gamma < 0 \end{cases}$$

or

$$u = \log \prod_{t=0}^{T} c_i^{\gamma \alpha^i}.$$

Let w_t be net worth at time t, and let c_t be consumption. Suppose there are n securities $1, 2, \ldots, n$ having gross rates of return $\rho_{t1}, \rho_{t2}, \ldots, \rho_{tn}$ in period t. Define

z_{t0}: Proportion of w_t consumed.

$(1 - z_{t0})w_t$: Amount invested.

z_{ti}: Proportion of $(1 - z_{t0})w_t$ invested in security i.

z_t: $(z_{t0}, \ldots, z_{tn})$.

ρ_t: $(\rho_{t1}, \ldots, \rho_{tn})$.

Assume $\rho_t \geq 0$ (limited liability), and that the ρ_t are intertemporally independent. Suppose that the investor possesses no source of income other than return on investment. Assume further that borrowing or short selling is allowed, with default occurring if $\sum_{i=1}^{n} z_{ti}\rho_{ti} < 0$.

(e) Show that $w_{t+1} = (1 - z_{t0})w_t R_{t+1}$, where $R_{t+1} = \max\{\sum_{i=1}^{n} z_{it}\rho_{it}, 0\}$.

Let $Z = \{z_t | 0 \leq z_t \leq 1, \sum_{i=0}^{n} z_{ti} = 1\}$ be the constraint set for all t. The investor's problem is

$$\max_{c}\{Eu(c_o, c_1, \ldots, c_T) | z_t \in Z, c_t = z_{t0}w_t\}.$$

For the power-law utility $U_{T+1} = \delta$ and $U_t = \delta \prod_{i=t}^{T} c_i^{\gamma \alpha^i} = c_t^{\gamma \alpha^t} U_{t+1}$. Let $f_t(w_t)$ be the maximum value of EU_t given w_t.

(f) Show that

$$f_t(w_t) = \max_{z_t \in z}(z_{t0}w_t)^{\gamma \alpha^t} E\rho_{t+1} f_{t+1}[(1 - z_{t0})w_t R_{t+1}],$$

with $f_{T+1} = \delta$.

(g) Show that the optimal policy for the power-law utility is

$$f_t(\mathbf{w}) = A_t w^{\lambda_t}, \quad \lambda_t = \gamma \sum_{i=t}^{T} \alpha^i; \quad z_{t0}^* = \frac{1}{\sum_{i=0}^{T-t} \alpha^i;}$$

z_{ti}^* solves $\max_{z_t \in Z} \delta E[R^{\lambda_{t+1}}](i = 1, \dots, n)$; and

$$A_t = \delta_{\lambda_t}^{-\lambda t} \prod_{i=t}^{T} (\gamma \alpha^i)^{\gamma \alpha^i} \prod_{i=t}^{T-t} E[R(z_i^*)^{\lambda_{i+1}}] \text{ for } t = 0, 1, \dots, T,$$

except that $A_T = \delta$ and $z_{Ti}^* = 0, i = 1, \dots, n$ [Hint: use backward induction.]

(h) Show that the optimal policy for the logarithmic utility is

$$f_t(\mathbf{w}) = A_t \log w + B_t; \quad z_{i0}^* = \frac{1}{\sum_{i=0}^{T-t} \alpha^i};$$

z_{ti}^* solves $\max_{z_t \in Z} \delta E[\log R](i = 1, \dots, n)$; and

$$A_t = \sum_{t=0}^{T-t} \alpha^i;$$

$$B_t = -A_t \log A_t + \log \alpha \sum_{i=t+1}^{T} \alpha^{i-t} A_t$$

$$+ \sum_{i=t+1}^{T} \alpha^{i-t} A_t \log R(z_{t-1}^*) \quad \text{for } t = 0, \dots, T,$$

except that $z_{Ti}^* = 0, i-1, \dots, n; \ B_T = 0$.

The solutions given above show that the optimal portfolio selection problem in each period requires the expected utility maximization of a single-period utility function with constant relative risk aversion r_t, in period t.

(i) Show that $r_t = 1 - \lambda_{t+1} = 1 - \gamma \sum_{i=t+1}^{T} \alpha^i$, with $\gamma = 0$ for the logarithmic case.

Note that risk tolerance increases or decreases with age accordingly as risk tolerance is greater or less than that of the logarithm.

(j) Show that for the power-law utility function, the optimal policy as $T \to \infty$ is

$$f_t(w) = A(\lambda)w^\lambda, \ \lambda = \frac{\gamma \alpha^t}{(1-\alpha)}; \ z_{t0}^* = 1 - \alpha;$$

z_{ti}^* solves $\max_{z \in Z} \delta E[R^{\alpha\lambda}], i = 1, \ldots, n$; and

$$A(\lambda) = \delta(1-\alpha)^\lambda \alpha^{\frac{\alpha\lambda}{(1-\alpha)}} \prod_{i=1}^{\infty} E[R(z_i^*)^{\lambda\alpha^i}] \text{ for all } t.$$

(k) Derive the optimal policy for the logarithmic case as $T \to \infty$.

[F20] (The Kelly Criterion: Additional properties)
Suppose ties are not allowed.

(a) Show there is a unique fraction $f_c > 0$ such that $G(f_c) = 0$, and $f^* < f_c < 1$.
(b) Show that G is a strictly concave function, and hence is strictly increasing from 0 to $G(f^*)$ on $[0, f^*]$ and strictly decreasing from $G(f^*)$ to $-\infty$ on $[f^*, 1]$.

The proofs of the next parts may be established using the Borel strong law of large numbers. Let S_t denote the number of successes in t Bernoulli trials. Then Borel's law is that $\Pr[S_t/t \to p] = 1$.

(c) Show that $G(f) > 0$ implies that $\lim W_t = \infty$ a.s.; i.e., for all $M, \Pr[\limsup W_t > M] = 1$.
(d) Show that $G(f) < 0$ implies $\lim W_t = 0$ a.s.
(e) Show that $G(f) = 0$ implies $\limsup W_t = \infty$ a.s. and $\liminf W_t = 0$ a.s.
(f) Show that $G(f_1) > G(f_2)$ implies $\lim(W_1(f_1)/W_2(f_2)) = \infty$ a.s.
(g) Interpret the results of (c)–(f).

[F21] (Generalized Kelly criterion)
Consider two investment strategies θ and θ^* having payoffs V_N and V_N^* after period N. These strategies are said to be

significantly different if and only if there exists $\varepsilon > 0, M$ such that for all $N > M$

$$\frac{1}{N} \sum_{n=1}^{N} E|\log V_n - \log V_n^*| > \varepsilon.$$

(a) Interpret this definition.

A set of strategies Ξ is bounded if and only if for all N and $\theta \in \Xi$ there exists $\alpha(\theta) < \infty$ such that $\theta \in \Xi$ implies

$$\frac{1}{N} \text{var} \sum_{n=1}^{N} \log V_n < \alpha(\theta).$$

(b) Interpret this assumption. Is it strong or weak?

(c) Show that Breiman's assumption that the random returns are finite and bounded away from zero is sufficient but not necessary for the satisfaction of the boundedness assumption.

(d) Use the Chebychev inequality to prove that for independent returns, a $\max\{E \log V_N\}$ criterion has a modified version of Property 1 (where convergence in probability replaces almost sure convergence) stated in Thorp's paper. Assume that all feasible strategies are bounded.

(e) Use the Chebychev inequality to prove that for dependent returns, a $\max\{E \log V_N\}$ criterion has the modified Property 1. Assume that all strategies under consideration are significantly different and bounded, and that the return distributions are independent of the investor's strategy.

(f) What can be said about Property 2 in Thorp's paper?

[F22] (The Kelly criterion and expected utility)

Suppose an investor's utility function is $u(W_T) = W_T^\alpha$, over period T wealth W_T, where $\alpha < 1, \alpha \neq 0$. Let the gross rate of return in each period t be r_t, where $r_t \equiv \sum r_i X_{it}$, the X_{it} are the relative investment allocations in period t, and the r_i are the gross rates of return for the individual investments assumed to be independently and identically distributed in time. Suppose $W_0 > 0$ is the investor's initial wealth; then his wealth at time T is

$$W_T = W_0 \prod_{t=1}^{T} r_t.$$

(a) Show that one may maximize W_T for fixed r_t by choosing the X_{it} so that in each period they maximize the expected logarithm of one period return, namely,

$$\max\left\{ E\log\sum_i r_i X_{it} \,\middle|\, \sum_i X_{it} = 1, X_{it} \geq 0 \right\}.$$

(b) Show that the optimal strategy, say X^l, is stationary in time i.e.,

$$X^l = (X_{1t}, \ldots, X_{nt}) \text{ for all } t.$$

(c) Show that with probability 1 the return under the strategy X^l is at least as high as under the strategy X^p, where X^p is the solution to

$$\max\left\{ E\left(\sum_i r_i X_i\right)^\alpha \,\middle|\, \sum_i X_i = 1, X_i \geq 0 \right\}.$$

Let us consider the expected utilities of strategies X^l and X^p.

(d) Find a distribution $F(r)$ and an α such that

$$\frac{E(r)^\alpha}{E\log r} = k > 1 \quad \text{for some specific } k.$$

Hence the power portfolio is better than the Kelly portfolio in terms of expected utility.

(e) Show that as $T \to \infty$ the power portfolio is infinitely better than the Kelly portfolio.

[**F23**] Consider the following continuous-time, deterministic consumption-investment problem. During the planning period $[0, T]$, a stream of income $m(t)$ and rate of interest $r(t)$ will prevail with certainty. A consumption plan $c(t)$ is a non-negative function on $[0, T]$. Assume that all assets (positive or negative) are held in the form of notes bearing interest at the rate $r(t)$. Assume also that initial asset holdings $S(0)$ are zero.

(a) Show that terminal assets (bequests) S are given by

$$S = \int_0^T \left[exp \int r(\tau)d\tau \right] [m(t) - c(t)]dt.$$

Assume that $r(t) = j$ for all $t \in [0, T]$. Define lifetime wealth M to be

$$M = \int_0^T e^{j(T-t)} m(t)dt.$$

(b) Show that

$$S = M - \int_0^T e^{j(T-t)} c(t)dt.$$

Assume that the consumer's preferences are given by a utility function $V = \int_0^T \alpha(t)g[c(t)]dt$, where g is the utility associated with the rate of consumption at any time, and $\alpha(t)$ is a subjective discount factor. Assume that g is strictly concave and twice continuously differentiable on $[0, \infty)$.

(c) If terminal wealth S has no utility, that is, if bequests are disregarded, show that the consumer's problem may be written as $\max_{S \geq 0} V$.

(d) Show that (c) may be written as

$$\max_c \left\{ \int_0^T \alpha(t)g[c(t)]dt \left| \int_0^T e^{j(T-t)}c(t)dt \right. \right.$$

$$\left. = M, c(t) \geq 0, t \in [0,T] \right\}.$$

(e) Show that a necessary and sufficient condition for c^* to be a solution to (d) is that

$$e^{j(T-t)}\alpha(t)g'[c^*(t)] = k \quad \text{for some } k > 0,$$

For all t such that $c^*(t) > 0$.

(f) Show that $e^{j(T-t)}\alpha(t)g'[c^*(t)] \leq k$ for $c^*(t) = 0$.

(g) Show that c^* is differentiable in the interior of the set $\{t|c^*(t) > 0\}$ if g'' is continuous and less than zero.

(h) Show that

$$\frac{dc^*(t)}{dt} = -\left\{ j + \frac{1}{\alpha(t)}\frac{d\alpha(t)}{dt} \right\} \frac{g'[c^*(t)]}{g''[c^*(t)]} \quad \text{for } c^*(t) > 0.$$

(i) Interpret the result in (h).

Assume that bequests S have utility $\phi(S)$, where ϕ is twice differentiable and strictly concave.

(j) Show the consumer's problem now becomes

$$\max_c \left\{ \int_0^T \alpha(t)g[c(t)]dt + \phi(S)|c(t) \geq 0 \quad \text{for all } t \in [0,T] \right\}.$$

(k) Show that a necessary and sufficient condition for c^* to be optimal is

$$e^{j(T-t)}\alpha(t)g'[c^*(t)] \leq \phi'(S) \quad \text{and}$$

$$c^*(t) = 0 \text{ when strict inequality holds.}$$

Here, $S^* = M - \int_0^T e^{j(T-t)}c^*(t)dt$.

(l) Formulate an algorithm for solving the problem in (k).

[F24] Consider a market with m regimes, n risky assets and a risk-free asset.

Let the vector of prices at time t be $P(t) = (P_0(t), P_1(t), \ldots, P_n(t))'$, where $P_0(t)$ is the price of the risk-free asset, with rate of return r_t at time t.

Let $Y_i(t) = \ln P_i(t), i = 0, \ldots, n$, be the log-prices. The price dynamics are within regime are defined by the stochastic differential equations: $dY_0(t) = r_t dt, dY_k(t) = \alpha_k dt + \Delta_k dZ$, with $Y_k(t) = (Y_{1k}(t), \ldots, Y_{nk}(t))', \alpha_k = (\alpha_{1k}, \ldots, \alpha_{nk})', \Delta_k = (\delta_{ijk}), dZ = (dZ_1, \ldots, dZ_n)'$, where $dZ_i, i = 1, \ldots, n$ are independent Brownian motions.

(a) Write out the wealth equation for a constant proportion investment strategy $X = (x_0, x_1, \ldots, x_n)$.

(b) Find the constant proportion investment strategy which solves $\max_x Ln(W(T))$.

[F25] Consider a pair of correlated arithmatic Brownian motions:

$$dY_1(t) = adt + b \cdot dW_1(t); X(0) = 0$$

$$dY2(t) = cdt + d \cdot dW_2(t); Y(0) = 0,$$

where $W_1(t)$ and $W_2(t)$ are two Brownian motions with $E[dW_1(t)dW_2(t)] = \rho dt$. Using an Euler scheme, simulate the evolution of the two arithmatic Brownian motions using the following sets of parameters:

- Short-time horizon:

Parameter		Set 1	Set 2	Set 3	Set 4
a		0.1	0.1	0.1	0.1
b		0.25	0.25	0.25	0.25
c		0.1	0.1	−0.1	−0.1
d		0.25	0.25	0.25	0.25
ρ		0.9	−0.9	0.9	−0.9
time interval	[0,1]	[0, 1]	[0, 1]	[0, 1]	
discretization δt	0.01	0.01	0.01	0.01	

- Long-time horizon

Parameter		Set 5	Set 6	Set 7	Set 8
a		0.1	0.1	0.1	0.1
b		0.25	0.25	0.25	0.25
c		0.1	0.1	−0.1	−0.1
d		0.25	0.25	0.25	0.25
ρ		0.9	−0.9	0.9	−0.9
time interval	[0,10]	[0,10]	[0,10]	[0,10]	
discretization δt	0.01	0.01	0.01	0.01	

What do you observe?

[F26] Consider the following pair of factor-driven processes.

$$dY_1(t) = aX(t)dt + b \cdot dW_1(t); X(0) = 0$$

$$dY_2(t) = cX(t)dt + d \cdot dW_2(t); Y(0) = 0,$$

where $W_1(t)$ and $W_2(t)$ are two Brownian motions with $E[dW_1(t)dW_2(t)] = \rho dt$.
The factor $X(t)$ follows the Ornstein–Uhlenbeck process:

$$dX(t) = -(X(t) - 0.10)dt + 0.25dW_X(t),$$

where $W_X(t)$ is a standard Brownian motion independent from $W_1(t)$ and $W_2(t)$.

Using an Euler scheme, simulate the evolution of the two arithmatic Brownian motions using the following sets of parameters:

- Short-time horizon:

Parameter		Set 1	Set 2	Set 3	Set 4
a		1.0	1.0	1.0	1.0
b		0.25	0.25	0.25	0.25
c		1.0	1.0	−1.0	−1.0
d		0.25	0.25	0.25	0.25
ρ		0.9	−0.9	0.9	−0.9
time interval	[0, 1]	[0, 1]	[0; 1]	[0, 1]	
discretization δt	0.01	0.01	0.01	0.01	

- Long-time horizon:

Parameter	Set 1	Set 2	Set 3	Set 4
a	1.0	1.0	1.0	1.0
b	0.25	0.25	0.25	0.25
c	1.0	1.0	−1.0	−1.0
d	0.25	0.25	0.25	0.25
ρ	0.9	−0.9	0.9	−0.9
time interval	[0,10]	[0,10]	[0;10]	[0,10]
discretization δt	0.01	0.01	0.01	0.01

(i) What do you observe?
(ii) What impact does the factor have?

Exercise Source Notes

Exercises [F1]–[F4] were provided by Bahsoun *et al.* (2013). Exercises [F5]–[F10] were provided by Thorp and Mizusawa (2013). Exercise [F11] is adapted from Ziemba–Vickson (1975): p. 664 # 5. Exercise [F12] is adapted from Ziemba–Vickson: p. 668 #10. Exercise [F13] is adapted from Ziemba–Vickson: p. 671 # 18. Exercise [F14] is adapted from Ziemba–Vickson: p. 672 # 19. Exercise [F15] is adapted from

Ziemba–Vickson: p. 677 # 2. Exercise [F16] is adapted from Ziemba–Vickson: p. 680 # 4. Exercise [F17] is adapted from Ziemba–Vickson: p. 681 # 5. Exercise [F18] is adapted Ziemba–Vickson: p. 690 # 14. Exercise [F19] is adapted Ziemba–Vickson: p. 694 # 21. Exercise [F21] is adapted from Ziemba–Vickson: p. 696 # 22. Exercise [F22] is adapted from Ziemba–Vickson: p. 696 # 23. Exercise [F23] is adapted Ziemba–Vickson: p. 697 # 25. Exercise [F24] is adapted from Ziemba–Vickson: p. 698 # 28. Exercises [F26] and [F27] were provided by Davis and Lleo (2013).

ABOUT THE AUTHORS

Dr. Leonard C. MacLean

Leonard MacLean is Professor in the School of Business Administration at Dalhousie University in Halifax, Canada. Dr. MacLean has held visiting appointments at Cambridge University, University of Bergamo, University of British Columbia, Simon Fraser University, Royal Roads University, University of Zimbabwe and University of Indonesia. From 1989 to 1995 he served as Director of the School of Business Administration at Dalhousie University. Professor MacLean's research focuses on stochastic models in finance, and models for repairable systems in aviation. He has published over 80 papers and co-authored three books. His papers appear in leading journals such as *Journal of Economic Theory, Journal of Economic Dynamics and Control, Quantitative Finance, Journal of Banking and Finance, Management Science, Health Services Research* and *Journal of Transportation and Statistics.* This work is funded by grants from the Natural Sciences and Engineering Council of Canada and the Herbert Lamb Trust. Dr. MacLean is the Editor of *Quantitative Finance Letters*. He teaches in the areas of statistics and operations.

Dr. William T. Ziemba

William T. Ziemba is the Alumni Professor (Emeritus) of Financial Modeling and Stochastic Optimization in the Sauder School of Business, University of British Columbia where he taught from 1968–2006. His PhD is from the University of California, Berkeley. He currently teaches part time and makes short research visits at various universities. At present he is the Distinguished Visiting Research Associate, Systemic Risk Centre, London School of Economics. He has been a Visiting Professor at Cambridge, Oxford, London School of Economics, University of Reading and Warwick in the UK, at Stanford, UCLA, Berkeley, MIT, University of Washington and Chicago in the US, Universities of Bergamo, Venice and Luiss in Italy, the Universities of Zurich, Cyprus, Tsukuba (Japan), KAIST (Korea), and the National University and the National Technological University of Singapore. He has been a consultant to a number of leading financial institutions including the Frank Russell Company, Morgan Stanley, Buchanan Partners, RAB Hedge Funds, Gordon Capital, Matcap, Ketchum Trading, and in the gambling area to the BC Lotto Corporation, SCA Insurance, Singapore Pools, Canadian Sports Pool, Keeneland Racetrack, and some racetrack syndicates in Hong Kong, Manila and Australia. His research is in asset-liability management, portfolio theory and practice, security market imperfections, Japanese and Asian financial markets, hedge fund strategies, risk management, sports and lottery investments, and applied stochastic programming. His co-written practitioner paper on the Russell–Yasuda model won second prize in the 1993 Edelman Practice of Management Science Competition. He has been a futures and equity trader and hedge fund and investment manager since 1983. He has published widely in journals such as *Operations Research, Management Science, Mathematics of OR, Mathematical Programming, American Economic Review, Journal of Economic Perspectives, Journal of Finance, Journal of Economic Dynamics and Control, JFQA, Quantitative Finance, Journal of Portfolio Management* and *Journal of Banking and Finance* and in many books and special journal issues. Recent books include *Applications of Stochastic Programming* with S. W. Wallace, SIAM-MPS, (2005), *Stochastic Optimization Models in Finance*, 2nd edition with R. G. Vickson, World Scientific (2006) and *Handbook of Asset and Liability Modeling*, Volume 1: *Theory and Methodology* (2006) and Volume 2: *Applications and Case Studies* (2007) with S. A. Zenios, North Holland, *Scenarios for Risk Management and Global Investment Strategies* with Rachel Ziemba, Wiley, (2007), *Handbook of Investments: Sports and Lottery Betting Markets*, with Donald Hausch, North Holland, 2008, *Optimizing the Aging, Retirement and Pensions Dilemma* with Marida Bertocchi and Sandra Schwartz (2010, 2015 (2nd edn.)) and *The Kelly Capital Growth Investment Criterion* (2010), with legendary hedge fund trader Edward Thorp and Leonard MacLean, *Calendar Anomalies and Arbitrage, The Handbook of Financial Decision Making* (with Leonard MacLean) and *Stochastic Programming* (with Horand Gassman), published by World Scientific in 2012 and 2013. In progress in 2015 is Handbook on the *Economics of Wine* (with O. Ashenfelter, O. Gergaud and K. Storchmann) and the Handbook *Futures Markets* (with T. Mallaris). He is the series editor for North Holland's Handbooks in Finance, World Scientific Handbooks in Financial Economics and

Books in Finance, and previously was the CORS editor of INFOR and the department of finance editor of *Management Science,* 1982–1992. He has continued his columns in *Wilmott* and his 2013 book with Rachel Ziemba have the 2007–2013 columns updated with new material published by World Scientific. Ziemba, along with Hausch, wrote the famous *Beat the Racetrack* book (1984), which was revised into *Dr Z's Beat the Racetrack* (1987), which presented their place and show betting system and the *Efficiency of Racetrack Betting Markets* (1994, 2008) — the so-called bible of racetrack syndicates. Their 1986 book *Betting at the Racetrack* extends this efficient/inefficient market approach to simple exotic bets. Ziemba is revising *BATR* into *Exotic Betting at the Racetrack* (World Scientific) which adds Pick 3, 4, 5, 6, etc., and provides updates to be out in 2016 with real bets he made across the world. Finally he has just completed *Travels with Dr Z: The Adventures of a Modern Renaissance Academic in Investing and Gambling,* a memoir and financial history of his investment activities over the last fifty years and *Great Investment Ideas,* which has all twelve of his applied investment papers published in the *Journal of Portfolio Management.* These hard to find papers cover many important topics including the evaluation of the greatest investors.

INDEX